Russia
IN PRIVATE

Russia
IN PRIVATE

Richard Yatzeck

Published by WriteLife, LLC
2323 S. 171 St.
Suite 202
Omaha, NE 68130
www.writelife.com

Printed in the United States of America

ISBN 978 1 60808 061 8

First Edition

"The Russians are a people who historically have needed a belief system to live by, whether Communism or Russian Orthodoxy... they have been uncomfortable with our notion... that the individual himself is left to develop philosophy, faith, and the meaning of life."

Hedrick Smith, <u>The New Russians</u>, p. xxvi

For George W. Smalley (1930-2003) and for the students

of Lawrence University who thumbed Skippy, ogled onion domes,

and, laughing, set up tents in the rain on the "Slavic Trips," 1969 to 1991.

TABLE OF CONTENTS

PREFACE

The account which follows embraces three kinds of Russian occasions, pretty much in chronological order. In 1961-2, I spent a year in Moscow as a graduate student, working on my dissertation. Between 1968 and 1997, I accompanied six groups of students and one group of alumni on tours of European Russia. In 1991 and 1997 I directed semester programs for the Associated Colleges of the Midwest-Great Lakes College Association in the south Russian city of Krasnodar. In between, I taught Russian literature at Lawrence University in Appleton, Wisconsin. Herein, I attempt to give form to my experience.

I believe that I have something to add to the ongoing discussion, in the Western press as in every Russian kitchen, of the two perennial questions: "Who is to blame?" and "What is to be done?" Both are book titles and the major questions regarding Russia's fate. My mite, however, in the sea of Russia discussion, does not pretend to *answer* these questions, but is rather an effort to describe the tea-and-vodka-ringed pine table over which these questions are raised: private Russia. As my Russian is decent, though not native, and my experience lengthy, I hope to be able to interest you mightily in this strange place which I have learned to love.

I do not intend to deal mainly with political matters as such. I will try, rather, to show what the Russia of my experience, between 1961 and 1997, has been able to teach me about a way of life quite foreign to, but not always less attractive than, the "certain certainties" of American and European culture.

When I return from Russia, ten times now since 1961, most people are utterly incurious about the place. "Why do you go there?" is the most frequent query. When I explain that I teach Russian literature, my reason seems sufficient, if esoteric. No more questions. There were two "questioners" at our basement apartment door three months after my first wife, Lois, and I returned in 1962. These FBI men queried, "Were you asked to be spies?" Then they warned: "Let us know if you are approached." They gave us a phone number.

That encounter was telling. Even the FBI was, essentially, incurious. They "knew," to the point of boredom, what Ronald Reagan thought when twenty-five years later he called the Soviet Union an "evil empire." Who would *want* to be a Russian spy? Hadn't the media made it clear that Russia was the most wretched, ghastly place on earth? Everyone *knew* all about Russia.

If the FBI had been interested, I could have given reasons for my interest in Russia. In an unhappy family, I read a lot: Turgenev, Dostoevsky, and Tolstoy included. In college one redhead and two films, *The Red Shoes* and *The Tales of Hoffmann* moved me from pursuing moneymaking engineering to the less promising humanities. German and Polish roots started me on languages. Labor union and Hungarian socialist friends pointed me east. What I really wanted was to belong to that warm, thoughtful world that

Turgenev seemed to represent, to escape the banal, dollar boosterism which, as I thought then, was all that America had to offer.

Now, fifty years later, I think that Russia was attractive to me because the characters of Turgenev, Tolstoy, and Dostoevsky were not exotic, but rather very close to the subsistence farmers who largely raised me. The excuses of sociology for human faults were simply beyond the pale of my models. Belief in taking responsibility for oneself in a difficult life was so prevalent in Genesee village that no one needed to brood upon it. When I chose Russia as my subject matter and as my career it was, I guess, because Russia was the closest thing to Genesee village that I had ever come upon, not because of my green Marxism.

My left-wing youth has mellowed, much too much, into middle-class comfort. Neither have I escaped the occasional foray into sociological excuse making. Still, for fifty years, private Russia has provided the generosity, idealism, and warmth which I hoped to find in her, as I found it on an eleven cow dairy farm in Wisconsin in the thirties. Perhaps, here, I will be able to convince you of this.

CHAPTER I

Moscow Exchange Year, 1961-62

My wife, Lois, and I arrived in Moscow by train via Paris, Prague, and Warsaw in September 1961. As I was in Moscow to write a dissertation on Maxim Gorky's dramaturgy, it should be clear that Orwell's *Homage to Catalonia* had not yet cured me of socialist romanticism. During a Fulbright year in Hamburg, an émigré Russian woman had indeed overcome much of my ignorance. At the same time, her warmth and the bewitching sounds of spoken Russian (we traded language lessons) made Russia as attractive as the Soviet Union had been to me, an ignorant, nineteen-year-old, self-styled Marxist. When I studied at Moscow State University, thanks to the cultural exchange treaty blessed by Nikita Khrushchev and Dwight D. Eisenhower in 1959, I was a card-carrying liberal. I'd voted for Adlai, gladly. If pushed, I would have admitted that I was in Russia to find a life, if not socialist, at least not aspiring to middle class. I gradually made out the features of such an existence - that's the secret thread here - and it was *not* socialist and not middle class either. Life for most Russians had little to do with such political and social distinctions at all. Neither socialist asceticism nor bourgeois consumption, in our sense, played any significant public role in 1961 Moscow.

Cultural consumption was another matter. My advisor's lectures on

Gorky and a desk at the Lenin Library comparable to Marx's nest at the British Museum made up my professional life. In the evening, though, Madison, Wisconsin, my cultural home until then, paled before the lively and various theatrical and concert life of Moscow. In his lectures, Professor Vysotsky seemed to imply that Gorky's dramas, like Lenin's electricity, had guaranteed a Communist future. However, he had a beautiful, pre-revolutionary academic accent, Polish "I" (which sounds like "w"). After four years of practice, I was just beginning to grasp spoken Russian, and his lectures, though socialistically dutiful, went down like Chopin. Then, privately, the professor suggested newer and more daring playwrights than Gorky, and arranged a week-long excursion to Leningrad, Peter the Great's "window on the West," for Lois and me. Once, when I visited him in the hospital, suffering from heart trouble, he insisted, like all Russian hosts, that I absolutely must share his hospital breakfast. This natural generosity I have found throughout the fifty years of my association with Russia and still utterly admire.

As regards evening activities, Khrushchev's denunciation of Stalin's crimes at the Twentieth Party Congress in 1956 had transformed, and at least partially liberated, the dramatic arts. One could choose Evgeny Shvarts's *The Naked King*, a relevant remake of "The Emperor's New Clothes," or Brecht's *Mother Courage*, though Brecht had always been suspect in Moscow. From the past, but by no means irrelevant, was all of Chekhov at the Moscow Art Theater, albeit in the turn-of-the-century Stanislavsky productions. *Swan Lake* or *Boris Godunov* in sumptuous settings at the Bolshoy Theater did not preclude performances of the more "formalist," then-recent works of Prokofiev and Shostakovich. These might be paired with Haydn, the "Farewell Symphony" with knee britches, wigs and candles, or even Corelli and Handel. My grandfather would have called this "God's own plenty," if one could imagine a nineteenth century lowland Scots teamster in 1961 Moscow. That is, I was occasionally aware of my impossibly good luck.

Our social life was equally varied. We had surprisingly little to do with the dozen other Americans studying at the Moscow State University, living in that Stalin "wedding cake" on the Vorobyov Hills that overlook Moscow to the north. We had a drink with one or another of our cohorts, a formal meeting if group needs were felt, but most of us, I think, tried to avoid situations where it would be natural to speak English. As two of the couples and a third wife were Scandinavian-born, we were an international group anyway. Also, the authorities had settled us in rooms rather far from each other in that hideous, comfortable skyscraper, happily mixed with the many other foreign students and students from the republics. Moscow Russians, who made up an unfairly large segment of the student body because of relatives important in the Party, were nevertheless seldom allowed to live at the university because they could reasonably commute to classes.

A Muscovite journalism student, Volodya, found us as soon as we arrived. He interviewed us for the student newspaper, became our guide and, I think, reported on our conversations to the KGB. This was bothersome, seemed false, then sad, and, finally, came not to matter at all. We were, after all, not secret agents, and had nothing to reveal but our obvious relative prosperity. Volodya took me to observe the municipal elections and the children's ballet that accompanied them at that balloting center. He told countless Radio Armenia jokes, which tended to turn upon the supposed homosexuality of all Armenians, until we found the civil courage to demur. Volodya also dared to show me the one-room communal "apartment" that he shared with his widowed mother. I suggest that he was taking a chance because the authorities tried to keep some distance between foreigners and Russian citizens.

Most of our Russian acquaintances arranged to meet us at quiet places and asked us not to dress too "American." I might have laughed at the simplicity of his one room, being from the country where, by definition, the streets are paved with gold.

Volodya's father, a zealous Communist in good standing, had been arrested in the post-WWII purges, and his family learned of his death only in 1959. Still, because no career was possible otherwise, Volodya was an ardent, if ironical, member of the Komsomol, getting out the vote at election time, neighing and braying properly at meetings. He gave me his textbooks on Marxism-Leninism, a required ten percent of the graduate curriculum, when I showed interest. He said that *he* certainly didn't intend to read them.

Another acquaintance that found *us* was the abstract painter and self-conscious hippy, *stilyaga* in Russian, Andrey. We had been asked by a student from the previous year's group to bring him drawing materials. Andrey, in turn, and his friend Sonia, threw a party to welcome us in their downtown apartment. Big band sound, rock, hadn't arrived yet; jeans and sweaters and beards and sandals were not present either. The revolutionary talk was not nearly as literate as that of my Hungarian high school friends

The walls were covered with Andrey's then-forbidden, rather nice abstract painting. When pushed, I *said* that the paintings were "rather nice." I realized too late that while this, though perhaps true, because the work was like that of fifty other painters lacking a particular *self,* should not have been said. I immediately became responsible for the U2 spy plane which had recently been shot down. Indeed, this was our first and last party with Andrey and the other *stilyagi,* but it did give us, in one evening, a quick view of their particular world of dissidence. Andrey had a three-room apartment, Levis, a good collection of jazz LPs, and was able to avoid employment, dodge the universal draft, and badmouth the regime because his father was an important party official. Most of his friends came from families of the *nomenklatura,* high ranking bureaucrats. As in the sixties in America, the revolt of the *stilyagi* was to a greater or lesser degree a generational conflict within the middle class.

At the university, our immediate neighbors and friends were an Uzbek couple, a Tadzhik bachelor, and a student of Russian literature from Lahore. These neighbors in the corridor, except for the man from Lahore, were much more pious about political matters. At least, they didn't allow themselves jokes at even Stalin's expense. Svet ("Light"), the Uzbek wife, spent long hours queuing to feed and clothe herself and her husband and taught us how to insulate our windows with cotton batting when zero weather came early. She was utterly grateful to have risen from her father's shepherd life.

The Tadzhik bachelor, Yurik, a mathematician, applied himself zealously in his courses and, like Svet, rejoiced at the chance to improve upon the fate of his father: a village school teacher. Indeed, even in 1961, it was mainly Muscovites who allowed themselves subversive "anekdoty," jokes about the absence of corn production or the bad quality of Russian beer, but then Muscovites, like New Yorkers, have traditionally sharp and biting tongues. In 1961 this quality was indulged privately. Publicly, among those with a career to make or lose, socialist correctness was predominant, as is political correctness in the United States.

Then there was the man from Lahore. Ari was a fine chef studying to be a professor of Russian, who received fresh spices and even special rice by Air India. His cousin was a pilot. He alone could occasionally beat Yurik at chess, which was played in the corridor lounge at every free moment. I like to think that Lois and I both loved him for his anciently correct English and fine manners, as well as for his dinners. One evening, Ari was visited by the eleventh-floor Komsomol (Young Communist) committee. They insisted upon verifying the cleanliness of his room. He bowed them in. After half an hour, unable to fault Ari's housekeeping, the tallest of the group reached up to find a very thin film of dust on the edge of the ceiling fixture. This he pushed under the chef's nose. Ari elegantly grasped the finger between two of his own and turned it over. A thick, black moon shone under the giant's fingernail. The Komsomol delegation had the grace to leave without a word.

Speaking generally, one applicant in ten was admitted to Moscow State University in 1961. (It must be remembered that Russia follows the European educational system in that "university" means graduate school. The place of our "college" is taken by the final years of certain elite middle schools.) Perhaps three out of ten graduate students were genuine Muscovites. Resident students, often from distant republics, were lucky to prepare for careers at this most prestigious of Russian graduate institutions. They were aware of their good fortune and worked accordingly. Foreign students like us, or Ari, or, say, the African students who, at that time, studied Russian at Lumumba University across town before coming to Moscow State, were not in the least impressed. The classrooms, laboratories, and physical living conditions, though exceptional in Russia, would have been unacceptable in Peoria or Addis Ababa. Some of the African students tended to let their disdain be known, and this, along with their assumption that socialism meant human equality, even to the point of dating Russian girls, led to racial incidents and, more than once, to murder. The western variety of ethnic or gender consciousness was literally unheard of in 1961. It had hardly developed, even in Moscow, by 1997. Russians, like many provincial peoples, have a surprising number of genuine democrats, but the majority has not learned the hypocritical necessity of hiding its racism for business or social reasons. Besides, Russian patriotism is heavily spiced with inferiority feelings toward a largely unknown, and thus threatening, overseas world. This makes racism there particularly vehement. The Iron Curtain played a role as well. Most Russians simply could not comprehend the material and social expectations of middle-class Africans or Asians.

Occasionally, perhaps at the theater, someone would overhear our

English and ask, "Is it true that you all have cars? Do you own a house? How many square meters of floor space?" By 1961, some Moscow Russians had serious doubts about a party line that ascribed the world's highest standard of living to Russia. After all that Marxist hype, after all those queues, *after all that dying*, didn't they deserve better? The Russians we met at the university or in downtown Moscow were as ignorant of our lives as we were of theirs, but they were *interested*, first of all, in material inequalities. Political discussion did finally take place once it appeared that we could be trusted. At that time, such conversation seldom took a dissident tone. Despite the Stalinist excesses that Khrushchev's 1957 revelations had made public, few Russians with whom we spoke could imagine anything but Soviet rule. While believing in elections, our friends tended to think that having more than one party would lead to anarchy. As far as personal rights were concerned, no one could really understand the concept of innocence until guilt is proven. Our acquaintances tended to take the not altogether unusual view, even here in the States, that murderers, thieves, and rapists would fill the streets unless they were kept behind bars until they had proved their innocence.

Much of our commerce with Russians involved a Baptist couple that Lois met at their church. The situation of Olga and Sergey may help to explain the situation of believers under late Soviet rule. Both had "engineering" degrees. "Engineering," in the Soviet Union, might mean extreme academic or industrial technical competence, but it could also mean work in food processing as the foreman of a canning line. Since Olga and Sergey were practicing Baptists, they could not expect to rise high on the technical career ladder. On the other hand, Sergey then wrote for and later became editor of the Baptist magazine *Brotherly Herald*. The four-hour services that we attended on Wednesday night or Sunday in the Moscow Baptist church were always crowded. We alone, not as inured to physical stress, were enjoined to share the one bench kept for foreign visitors. The congregation stood, perhaps eight hundred people. This was the only Baptist church in Moscow, but Sergey told me that there were twelve million Baptists in Russia at that time. (It may be of interest that while Olga's mother was a Baptist, her father, the manager of a small factory, was a member of the Communist Party.) There certainly must have been ten times as many practicing Orthodox believers; for there were a number of "working" Orthodox churches in Moscow then, and we visited some of them. The services were long, and the congregations, of all ages and genders, stood throughout. This was not primarily because of a lack of space, but rather because it is a cardinal assumption of Russian Orthodoxy that the body is tried for the soul's sake. Exceptions were made for the very old and the infirm. While the Baptists sang hymns that we were used to in the States, the music of Orthodoxy was exotic, medieval, full of minors, and grand. The icon screen which mediates between this material world and the world of the spirit, the veneration of special images for various ills and afflictions, the mixture of rich incense and fat candle-smoke from thin, yellow-brown candles all seemed, to us, not only exotic, but strangely moving. Particularly impressive, musically, were the chants of an all-night Easter service in the cathedral of the Old Believers, a large sect which broke from the state church in the seventeenth century.

I dwell upon church matters, though an agnostic, because most Americans seem to think that Communism was successful in throttling religion. In truth, this proved to be beyond the power of even Stalin, though the church saw better and worse times. Many believers suffered exile or death, and many church buildings were desecrated or destroyed. In 1961, the impossibility of material economic advancement, which did not mean starvation, was the price that our Baptist friends paid for their beliefs. For us, this would be an extremely heavy price to pay. Olga and Sergey seemed to find it insignificant, and they were by no means grim and humorless or lacking in physical needs and desires. They were, I guess, simply genuine Christians.

Only once, some time in the 1980s, did Sergey try to evangelize me, though he was a preacher, and a powerful one, besides being an editor. At that time, the Russian Baptists were allowed to send a delegation to a church congress in St. Louis. Then Sergey, having seen the many *things* Americans live among and with and for, feared for my soul. I managed to convince him that success didn't mean much to me, and he ceased his direct efforts. During another visit, I found him in the hospital. Preparing hurriedly for a further overseas congress, he neglected a "stomachache" which resulted in peritonitis. "As it happens," he said with a grin, "my life was saved by American antibiotics, the first shipment this hospital has been able to obtain. Although I haven't been able to save your soul, you have saved my life." Sergey then went on to inform me that this was the very hospital to which Lenin was brought, in the '20s, when he was shot by Fanya Kaplan. "Just look," he

21

grinned, wickedly, "what piety! They haven't even changed the wallpaper, and it's been sixty years." It is true that even Sergey wouldn't have joked so in 1961, or even in 1969.

When asked a direct question, it is Sergey's way to take one seriously. Unfailingly, he begins with *"Seychas, minutochku,"* one moment, please. He thinks, then he gives you his best possible answer. On the occasion when I found him in the hospital, I was vetted first at the Baptist church office. Even in the early '80s, Russians didn't always absolutely *need* foreign visitors. Then, after the obligatory lunch, good cabbage soup and black bread and butter, with the church staff, a secretary, Vera Petrovna, called a taxi and took me to Sergey's hospital. On the way we passed the Lubyanka, the KGB building, and Vera murmured: "Such an *unhappy* building." Later, when Sergey mentioned working with the Metropolitan, the head of the Russian Orthodox Church, I asked, as I needn't have, "Do you kiss his ring?"

"Seychas, minutochku," came the traditional reply. "Yes, I do. Whom do *you* bow to, Dik?"

Both Vera's remark about the "unhappy" KGB headquarters, and she meant *elementally* suffused with misfortune, and Sergey's response to my question, which implied, of course: "Everyone bows. The question is, to whom? " express what I find special, characteristic about Russia, or about some Russians. For now, I'll just call this thing "high seriousness." It is a characteristic that I deeply admire and need.

During the winter of 1961, Lois had found it possible to visit Zagorsk, then the site of the only functioning Russian Orthodox seminary, and to interview the Metropolitan, supreme head of the Orthodox church in Russia. To her general questions about the state of the church she received bland and optimistic replies. She was given a private tour of the seminary's especially rich collection of icons, altar cloths, and other ritual appurtenances. The collection, chronologically arranged, large, valuable and full of rarities, was sufficient to suggest that the governments of Lenin and Stalin, no matter how ideologically atheistic, had been unable, or had felt it unfeasible, to attempt to destroy all vestiges of Russia's thousand-year history of Orthodoxy.

For most of our nine months in Moscow, the university, where we lived, could be entered only by showing a pass with a photograph. As we compared the life of the streets with the university conveniences, living quarters, stores, theaters, and restaurants, it seemed likely to us that the passes were required to avoid a sudden sharp rise in the population of the university complex. We were, indeed, a much-coddled segment of the Moscow population. More than a few of the students managed to smuggle in families rather too large for the two-person suites, at least from an American point of view.

Nevertheless, sequestration wore upon us. However, long before we were absolutely thirsting to quit Moscow, May arrived. Spring was suddenly, warmly present. Life seemed to open up. Lois and I trekked to Gorky Street to watch the May Day parade, the prime celebration of Soviet pride and power. (Christmas had been marked mainly by the appearance of Algerian oranges in the markets, received in return for tanks, but still costing a Russian day's salary apiece.) As the avenue was already teeming with early arrivals, we climbed a tall, iron gate and perched on the blunted spears at the top to watch the show. After the goose-stepping regiments and the tractor-drawn ballistic missiles, the procession became more humane. Factory, farm, and mercantile collectives made up by far the largest segment of the three-hour column. Their banners bore, for the most part, the all too official "Peace and Friendship" slogan, but the people seemed genuinely friendly. The leaders of one collective spotted us on our perch, and with hand gestures and friendly cries invited us to join them. In this way, two Americans were part of the column reviewed by Khrushchev and Co. in Red Square, in front of Lenin's tomb, on May Day 1962.

On the tram going home, a drunken Red Army major refused to produce a ticket, claiming that "the Red Army rides free on May Day." The not hulking uniformed lady conductor simply seized him by collar and belt and threw him into a muddy cross street. This seemed a surprising but sufficiently democratic conclusion to the holiday that President Eisenhower, never a great radical, renamed "Law Day" in the States.

May brought not only a softening of irongray winter, but also of the concierges who guarded the university doors. They stopped asking for passes. Their sliding windows were often simply empty: they'd found better things to do in the spring weather. This made us think that we might consider entertaining outside friends, a forbidden pleasure until now. The Iron Curtain seemed to be relaxing with the coming of summer.

The American and British embassies greatly cushioned our experience of Soviet reality. Their clubs, pubs, and mailing facilities were put at our disposal. A small grocery store stocked with Scandinavian imports in the basement of the U.S. Embassy absolutely electrified our otherwise Russian bill of fare. We had gone caroling with the two embassies' singers, attended the U.S. ambassador's New Year's Eve reception as invited guests and were generally looked after. Our group wanted, at least symbolically, to return some fraction of this generosity. Sharing the feeling of spring thaw, we asked the university for permission to entertain those members of the British and American embassy staff who had been most friendly and helpful. We planned a small reception and a tour of the premises.

As it happened, none of the embassy people had ever been allowed into Moscow State. In contrast with our more or less ignored existence in the Soviet capitol, they were guarded in their compounds and followed when they traveled or simply went to work, and their telephones were tapped. All of our mail that came through the Russian post office was opened. (I once had a postal clerk apologize because a letter had not been glued shut again.) In any event, the friends, whom we were foolish enough to invite before we had university approval, looked forward to crossing at least one forbidden boundary: the portals of Moscow State University.

As it turned out, our *starosta,* "eldest" or group leader, was informed that our request was refused. Since we had already invited our friends, we were embarrassed and doubly angry. This was our first experience of a serious *nyet,* sheltered creatures that we had been. There was nothing to do but inform our guests of our failure. They were, as they had been all year, most understanding. We were enraged. We wanted vengeance.

At about the same time that we requested permission for a reception, we presented our proposed schedule for the two-week tour of the country. This tour was a part of President Eisenhower's student exchange contract with Secretary Khrushchev. We asked, on the advice of the geographer who was one of our group, to visit Central Asia (Tashkent, Samarkand and Bukhara), Azerbaijan (Baku), Georgia (Tbilisi), Armenia (Erevan and Lake Sevan) and the Ukraine (Kiev). Our wish list was granted, with the exception of Bukhara, as Aeroflot had no flights to that city.

I assume that the geographer was the one person in the group with anything but the crudest notion about even the location of Bukhara. Our initial choices had been limited to "open" areas, and much of the Union was closed to foreign travel. (The U.S. State Department, quite correctly assuming that one could deal with the Soviet government only in terms of a strict *quid pro quo,* had responded to "closed" areas by superimposing a map of the Union on a U.S. map and closing those areas where Soviet closed zones fell. Thus, Soviet students could visit Manhattan, but not Brooklyn, Gary, but not Chicago.) In any event, Bukhara was an "open" city. Simmering because of our aborted party, we announced that we would accept no journey that did not include Bukhara. We warned that we would release this decision to the American press.

This decision was, of course, not taken without dissension. A few wiser heads among us, not mine, wondered if we wanted to risk our one chance to see the larger Union, for this was long before today's widespread tourism. Still, democrats that we were, the stubborn, angry majority ruled and, as it happened, won. Bukhara was included in our tour by commandeering the official plane of a local Party bigwig. We traveled in the sofas that ringed the lovely Bukhara rug in the middle of the passenger compartment. I suppose, now, that the exchange program seemed valuable enough to the Russians to put up with our blackmail. After nine months of being agreeable, we suddenly realized that we had *clout*. Still, I don't really know why the Russian authorities gave in. The lesson seemed to be that one could, on occasion, reverse a seemingly concrete *nyet*.

The journey itself was memorable because it brought us to just a few of those myriad areas in the Union where Russian culture and the Russian language were merely tolerated, on sufferance. We knew, abstractly, that <u>Pravda</u> appeared in more than one hundred languages daily, most of them not Russian, or even Slavic. Still, the cerulean blue tile mosques of very Muslim Tashkent, the faceted stone churches of Tbilisi which preached Christianity five hundred years before Russia's acceptance of Orthodoxy in 988, the citizen of Erevan who pointed out "our" mountain, Ararat, far to the west in Turkey now, even the softer speech and manners of Ukrainian Kiev, made the Union's variety real. It was a special pleasure to speak our still very imperfect Russian with people to whom the language was also a second language, foreign. They made us sound pretty good.

As the proverb has it: "Moscow is far, and God is high above: I'll do what I like." We found honest and open conversation much easier to manage in these ethnic republics. As Andrey Amalrik was to suggest in the book *Will the Soviet Union Survive Until 1984*, the conversation turned often upon questions of local sovereignty. An Intourist guide in Georgia, showing us with great pride a museum of magnificently enameled, silver-mounted icons, assured his audience that Georgians were all atheists now, and then then added, "Of course, we were evangelized, civilized, five hundred years before those northern barbarians." Our surprise at the collapse of the Communist regime in 1991 may have been nothing compared to the Russian surprise at the disaffection of their non-Russian republics.

A bright memory from our farewell excursion obtrudes. We were, I remember, in the south, in Tbilisi, and were offered an evening outing to an ancient Greek theater. There had, in ancient times, been Greek colonies all along the Black Sea coast.

We went as a group in an ancient bus and then walked several hundred yards to the crest of a low ridge. Below us lay, in the reddish stone of the region, a perfect, and perfectly round, orchestra for the actors. The crescents of stone benches for perhaps a thousand viewers rose toward us. The theater seemed all complete in the evening light, neither cracks nor gaps showing. It felt, in this eastern land, very like our western home.

I remembered then a young couple, met that day in the elevator of our hotel, who proudly carried their little son. "What is his name?"

They looked at me and asked, "Are you American?"

I nodded.

"His name," they said, in 1961, during strict Socialism, "his name is *Azad*. It means 'Freedom.' It is a very old Armenian name." And they laughed, winked, and left.

Now, in this old theater, as in the elevator, one felt the fragility of the satrapy, indeed, of any fixed political arrangement, and that the world, even here, in this corner of the Union, was large and as fluid as the sea. This was not a feeling often experienced in the old Union.

The thickness of the "Iron Curtain," in 1961, may be suggested by the following anecdote: in Paris, outside Notre Dame, Lois and I bought a foot-high plaster gargoyle, its fangs deep in a dog, or a baby. We carried it with us to Russia, not trusting the mail home. The cleaning lady whom we saw once a week for nine months asked us, near the end of our stay, if that "Satan" on the bookcase was our god. That she was perfectly serious indicates the mental, cultural, even chronological gap between the United States and Russia in 1961 or 2012 for that matter. I forget how we answered, but the question was a poignant one. Lois and I, it was becoming clear, worshipped different gods.

CHAPTER II

Wisconsin to St. Petersburg

...The German cried "Then why the devil are you riding through this poisonous land against the Turks?" The marquis smiled. "In order to return."

Rilke's *Cornet*

I don't know what we could have been thinking of. George Smalley, my senior colleague, learned *his* Russian in the military crash program at Syracuse. Then, he'd fallen in love with Prague School linguistics at the University of Chicago. My Russian came from the University of Madison, Wisconsin and from nine months in Moscow in '61 on the government exchange program. We wanted, I guess, to plunge our 60's students, theoretical radicals in large part, into the real grit of socialism, to guide them to the point from which they could "kill their own lion" as George, operatic as always, had put it in a much-quoted graduation speech.

I'm a comparative literature type, rather too prone to roleplaying in foreign cultures, sure that literature will somehow make sense of life. George, more scientific, drove and led our common students to develop a system of Russian grammar without irregular forms, a smoothly functioning set of rules to straighten Russian's interminable meanders. Neither of us had time for academic politics, both scorned mere "advancement." Finally though, we were both mesmerized by a country, a culture, utterly foreign to our U.S., Midwestern expectations. As Susan Richards wrote:

What was it that I should have known about Russia, about myself, before I embarked on this journey? I tried to explain what had been happening; how every day I seemed to understand less and less of what went on around me, how the ordinary transactions of life worked ... "Understand!" this mild-mannered man broke in, incensed at the word. "You are speaking like a Westerner! Logically! But life here is not logical! Understanding immobilizes! Once you understand the problem here you know that it is irremediable. It is better not to understand too much if you want to remain free to act."

There was nothing more to say.

***

We in the West believe in problem solving. Every day discovers a Thomas Edison or Henry Ford of maturation, marriage counseling, monetary success, sexual expertise, a love or a death guru. George and I were fascinated by the essentially innocent absurdity of Raskolnikov's desire to be Napoleon, the irresolvable nature of Anna Karenina's passion: by the rich stasis of nineteenth century Russian culture, where everything is hopeless, yet vital beyond the iron theories of Bentham, Darwin, or Malthus, certainly beyond the cheap absurdities of our own Norman Vincent Peale.

Repelled by America's overwhelming prosperity, but hypocritical enough to enjoy it at times, we were attracted, as our students also have been, by the buoyancy, generosity, and sheer verve of this people whose virtues become most evident in disaster. Then again George, largely English by descent, prided himself on some mysterious admixture of Gypsy blood, and a need to wander. I wanted the sheer pleasure of speaking Russian again; eight years having passed since my stint in Moscow on the government exchange. Perhaps it is the different mask or role that goes with the use of a foreign language that attracts me. A fierce opponent of "selfesteem" education, I have, nevertheless, little enough of that element in my everyday American existence. Whatever the case, whether the basic cause was curiosity about Russia, Gypsy blood or a desire for theater, one bright October day in 1967, drinking coffee at the student union, we dreamed up a camping tour of eastern (now central) Europe and Russia. George's appetites were vast. He convinced me that we needed not a normal ten week term, but a full fifteen week summer, to "do," which was, of course, suspiciously American, all eastern Europe, Russia and Istanbul as well, that source of Russian Orthodoxy, site of Hagia Sophia, Holy Wisdom, the mother church.

I don't remember just how we sold Dean Francis Broderick on the junket, but I can guess. George, who had sold books, hawked paint and could have merchandised hourglasses in the Sahara, was certainly the effective source of our success. He had impenetrable, thorny eyebrows, absolutely Tartar cheekbones, and the certain, piercing glint of a seer or shaman. In George's urgent presence, the Dean might have been convinced to buy a moonwalk. Dr. Broderick knew, too, that George spent fifty hours a week haranguing his linguistic troops and had never paid any attention to the officially prescribed six-hour-a-week teaching requirement. Whatever program he touted, George would most certainly do more than his part. As it turned out, we easily got the go-ahead from the president and faculty to sleep in slavic swamps for the summer of '69.

Alexander Lipson of MIT was, at that time, running summer tours of the Soviet Union for high school students. Another Prague School adept, he agreed to schedule and equip a tour for us as well. He came to Lawrence to explain his touring procedures, lectured and demonstrated traveling light in the East. One shirt, two pair of socks, Woolite, dried fish from peasant markets, all personal possessions to fit in one small suitcase: 15" x 28" x 4". We would travel and live in used VW vans carrying tents, sleeping bags, propane burners, and kitchen equipment. We rode seven students to a van, leaving room for the obligatory two Intourist guides. Each bus kept a daily account of purchases. A mechanic's van with spare parts and a bookkeeper completed our six-machine fleet.

We got right off the plane from Chicago and into these buses at the Brussels airport, and then dropped the vehicles back in Brussels fifteen weeks and fifteen thousand miles later. Every day we rotated as navigators and drivers, teaching the intricacies of the stick shift to the uninitiated. Our students blossomed in this hard, unaccustomed school, certainly because Lipson had spent a good few years perfecting his system. When we began our trip, in 1969, it was possible to set the same price for a summer in eastern Europe, as Lawrence charged for an elevenweek term, and to offer the same three credits, one having been earned in advance in a special linguistics course for the languages other than Russian that we would meet. The other two credits were for conversational Russian and a trip journal. The students themselves researched and produced travel and language guides.

Our itinerary ran more or less as follows: Brussels, Finland, the Soviet Union; Leningrad to Odessa to Kiev; Poland, Czechoslovakia, Austria, Hungary, Rumania, Bulgaria, Turkey, Yugoslavia, Brussels; a great, meandering loop through Eastern and Central Europe. George, leader and autocrat, *samoderzhets,* was urban and hasty. I, an avoider, too seldom willing to quarrel, preferred rural and slow, but kept up as best I could. The pace was exhilarating.

We did this tour, with minor or major changes, twelve times between 1969 and 1991. Cost increases, easier opportunities to visit and study in the Soviet Union, the breakup of the bloc, then of the Union, a quite new prevalence of crime in the East, our own aging, all contributed to the trip's demise. We had had a good, long run.

The incidents that follow, largely sketches from my trip journals, will follow our itinerary as much as possible. The account then concludes with a Krasnodar semester in 1991, an alumni tour on the Upper Volga and another Krasnodar semester in 1997. Its connecting theme: what the Russians had to teach us about living. Our summers in the East made the Slavic trip the beginning of a lifelong passion for Eastern European survival culture for George, for me, and by their own testimony, for a majority of our 300-plus student traveling companions. This book is for them, in fulfillment of a promise to sometime write a work entitled *The Cheap Cafes of Eastern Europe* which Matt, one of our students, prophesied and proposed years ago.

***

"But you *do* know," an East German teacher once said to me, "which side you are on." As I seemed to be at the midpoint of what Hemingway called the classical swing from left to right, I didn't honestly have a side to be on. Nevertheless, because Herr Doktor Bauer needed to believe in the existence of conviction *somewhere,* I hypocritically agreed that the way of the "free world" was best. Though this was fifty years ago, I find that I still have not finished with the question.

Seven times, once every four years beginning in 1969, I took part in Lawrence University's Slavic Trip. This served to keep my Russian somewhat current, but its greatest value was that it removed me from my usual summer rut. Instead of exchanging tractoring for beef on a dairy farm, I was brought cheek to jowl with my students. All about us lay my subject matter: Russia. On days when we switched camps, I sat in a VW bus for eight or twelve hours a day with six of my students. Then, for a day or two, I lived in a Russian campground or motel, and spent the days "doing" Leningrad, Turgenev's estate, or a Black Sea beach, when the adolescent desire to roast on rocks became strong among the troops. In rain or baking weather, there was no good place to read a book. There were amazingly few administrative matters to deal with. I had somehow to endure the bottomline realities of my students and myself in farthest Slavia. I was not always pleased with the students or myself. They once even voted me out of one of their buses. Russia and the students did teach me, although I'm not a quick study.

My colleague and eternal enemy, George Smalley, seemed to love and enjoy students. I found them, in certain moods, amazingly ignorant and, worse, autistically self-immersed. My Marxist youth saw them, largely bourgeois and suburbanite, as the products of a wealthy, wasteful, plastic and, necessarily, a declining culture. Nine months of Russian life in 1961, however, had given my Marxist youth a severe battering. Class judgments never came quite so easily after my dissertation stint in Moscow, though they did, and do, still come. I will try, here, to show how the students and Russia nudged me toward other kinds of judgments, albeit not final ones. Which side *am* I on?

***

We traditionally left Appleton on the morning of graduation. Once George even interrupted that holiest of academic ceremonies to gather the troops and leave early as we hadn't been able to arrange a later flight. Although one may, certainly, discuss the nature of true education, George was forever more than ready to let our colleagues and administrators feel that only "out there," in Russian reality, could anything really be learned. Not everyone took this in good part. Luckily, our critics couldn't know that trip preparations, given the approach of graduation and the ritual sufferings of final exams, were usually incomplete. We were always more or less unready.

In Chicago, George left me to charm parents arriving early to see their sons and daughters off. He disappeared into an O'Hare pub for a couple of manhattans. A Chicago friend, Frank, my college roommate, helped me. With the aid of parents, slivovitz, and then a mixture of the two, we transferred cases of peanut butter and ketchup from parental cars to unbelieving Sabena freight handlers. The slivovitz somehow cancelled out the offensive peanut butter. The parents were excited about adventures ahead for their offspring and, for a bit, wished that they could go along. They trusted me and the now-returned George in a child-like way, perhaps because we spoke with automatic Russian accents and weary authority, both taken from old movies. Three missing passports magically appeared at the final boarding gate, and we were off.

George and I, depression kids, never quite believed that we were on our way to Europe. The students, who have been flying since birth, were more blasé and snoozed. We couldn't sleep, so we flirted all night with the Polishborn flight attendant. She brought us extra dinners and cognac, gratis, and we imagined ourselves to be cunning eastern European operators. We ostentatiously refused to watch the American film.

When our jet met the dawn, our Polish cutie had seventyfive passengers to serve while five flight attendants served thirty businessmen in business class. She was armed with blue, shiny, aluminum make-up, small eyes, one squinting, and her anger. The sound for the film hadn't functioned, the john was super-tiny and not very clean, the food less than so-so. Jet steerage? A white-haired man demanded and got a real flute for his champagne. Who am I to complain about *any* trip to Europe, son of a good man though a failed chiropractor, grandson of a drunken, loving plumber? Any flight will do just fine.

Brussels at noon. Our advance crew, led by Greg, had the VW buses packed with tents, camp stoves, dried soup, French bread, and Edam cheese.

We bulled through a jet-lag-dogged drive to Holland and our tents were initiated that first afternoon behind a dike. I rose earlier than the others to the sound of a cuckoo, dropped my tent, took a morning shower, and enjoyed a brisk walk. Underway, old woodsman that I am, I realized that the sun was sinking in the west, not rising in the east, and that I had utterly lost track of time and direction. I rolled my sleeping bag under the bus and went back to sleep. The students woke me when our first genuine European morning arrived. Mistakes of time and direction abound in me, it seems.

We visited Bruges first, and then Amsterdam. We'd hardly heard of Bruges, but knew it meant neat bridges, which it certainly did. It was a tight little town, preserved with much effort, but preserved! Damn the automobile! There was a quiet, mossy-treed park with Flemish and Latin tags on the trees, Queen Astrid's Park, a subtle jewel.

The students on my bus were Stephanie and solid, gentle, Cindy, afraid of me from her sister's tales out of class. She asked "stupid," good questions like "Why brick houses? Why pointed roofs? What do Belgians *do*?" Then there was Jane, quiet and not used to smiling, plugged into her Walkman, scared? Steve was large and generous, smiling, and Kevin, a good, active, unshaven sort. Dawn, a genius at Russian, was more open with others than I would have imagined, kept careful books, and read maps most exactly. Good! Good bunch, it seemed. George passed us rapidly in *his* bus: how jealous of sovereignty, forever a child, I guess. Who *cares* who's boss? (Did *I*, sometimes?)

We cruised the flat, small fields of Belgium and Holland. There were one or two people cultivating potatoes and cabbages, by hand, in utterly level, closely hedged acres. Two thirds of the landscape is sky, as in Ruysdael. Two men and a dog were walking out to their barge in low water, rather far inland but still tidal. Hip boots. Everything ditched and drained. This hay - Sudan grass? Why were the cows so clean? One saw a few more horses than at home and small flocks of sheep, subsistence farming still, which seems the only real life.

That evening in Amsterdam, we were involved in a long search for the island campground somewhere near the middle of the city. This town was like an honorable, bourgeois house with angry, disorderly children. Graffiti on a water tower, writ large: "Kill the Poor!" Tired, hungry, we roared with laughter. Was it funny in its utter outrageousness? (We hardly picked up on the irony.)

Having found the campground, which was full of crowing pheasants, we got a lecture on the evils of marijuana as the camp director absentmindedly rolled himself a joint, then directed the kids to "The Bulldog" tavern where, this season, the action was said to be. They returned, bored, early enough to die laughing as they put up tents in a rain so heavy that there was, clearly, no longer a reason to put up tents. Super nice, that laughter. May we always meet discomfort so.

Lovely in their endurance, the students do always strike me as amazingly young. That their age remains constant, while mine doesn't, must certainly be one of the problems. As I got beyond their names and obvious features, I found that I was accompanied by a vegetarian couple who set the eating tone for the rest, and a born again slick operator who, quite unjustly, was letter perfect at the guitar and the Russian language: an artist and a poet. They were all, naturally, Americans. I am a hardened chameleon. Because I supposed myself to have learned from bad experience: the bad experience of students with me, I decided not to drive the bus unless absolutely necessary. I would let these students discover Europe without the aid of my vast expertise. However, if I am not teaching and leading, I don't know what to do with myself among students. I tried to listen. They seemed amazingly young.

I always forget that they are, in public at least, pack or peer group animals, and democratic to boot. When they sing, they sing sad and selfpitying songs with lyrics like "I am a Rock, I am an Island." This is irritating. Why don't they sing Russian songs? It may be because they don't know any. Mainly though, because "good" music and "good" books and "good" conversations are classroom demanded things. At their age, they need to rebel against what an older and, from the look of the world, not very wise generation demands. They need to belong to their own generation. Still, until I learn better, I act as if they must be, maybe socratically, guided to my truth, my good. The bus was not very comfortable.

It was physically uncomfortable. Seven people, with occasional guests and tour guides, had to live in that tin box for fourteen weeks. Luggage, much too much, food, utensils, spare tires, an extra windshield; we needed order. I tried not to insist, but became enraged. My controlled bile at odd socks coated with peanut butter, loose pages of travel guides and dirty dishes, was certainly worse than open anger. I traded the role of voluble pedagogue for that of a silent, implacable judge. All this took about two days.

By now, we were passing Hamburg where the kids were generous enough to drop me at a friend's house, although my bad directions cost them half a day's travel time. Dieter and Frieda gave them coffee and pastry, an insider's view of what to see up north in brick-Gothic Lubeck, and maps from Dieter's insanely large collection. I would catch them in three days in Sweden. Teacher and students were relieved at the break, I think.

Hamburg took me, in time, back to my own youth, as a Fulbright exchange teacher and student. My friend Dieter, five years older than I, remarked on the wholesome, intelligent, brisk quality of my students. His children, one rebel in particular who is my godson, are managing to be both banal and corrupt, irresponsible, messy, socialistic and what? *Young.* I took the part of Gerd and Reinhardt, defended the "greens" and the antiwar movement, *understood* his children though I was somehow incapable of forgiving my students their youth, and got into one hell of an allnight argument with Dieter, their father, my old friend. Himself a Fulbright scholar and erstwhile noisy heckler of Joe McCarthy, he regarded the present antiwar meeting, which was tying up downtown Hamburg, as of a piece with the bad manners, dress, thought, and culture of his children. Reinhardt, on the upstairs piano, tactfully played Beatle songs and Beethoven by turns. If he was fiddling while his father burned, he was doing it with ability and tact. Dieter, unhearing, blamed me for his sons' politics, music, and nonchoice of careers. Would I ever grow up? I was doubtful and not very repentant either.

As George was with our bus cavalcade, I took three days in Hamburg.

Long, spacious flatland walks, Westphalian ham, the return of grammatical German, all placed me, also *vis-à-vis* Dieter, back at the age of twentytwo. Then this experienced European tried to talk sense to a raw Wisconsin romantic. I was sobered, but hardly reformed, when Dieter and Frieda, according to that lovely continental custom, warmly saw me off on the overnight train to Sweden.

In Linkøping, Sweden, where I caught the troops, Øke and Margaret Anderson, complete strangers, had heartily taken in a busload of us because they had relatives in Chicago. Good, generous people, they included me, too. There turned out to be a dance nearby on Saturday night, so we went, the students taking the "family" car. The Andersons and I arrived later, after an elderly bout of Norwegian herring and Finnish vodka. My morning antiAmerican feelings, about littering, a rarity here, were balanced by evening second thoughts as Margaret, who speaks not English but German, described the difficulties of *Swedish* life: no litter, no advertising on the roads, but many social problems. They, as responsible officials, Øke a manager who rents out apartments, Margaret a clerk for the Nykøping police, dared not be seen drinking or dancing anywhere in their home town. So even Swedish *officials* spent their Saturday where they weren't known. What unfreedom!

The dance was a great success although Margaret was interested in learning the Twist from *me*. The students all found Swedish partners, changed every two dances, met a tipsy Finn whose one phrase was "I love Americans" (*girls*, he meant, and they really are called *flicka* there) and felt, I think, accepted for once; successful evening, though Øke did have a hard time bringing himself to ask Jeannie Knight to dance. All Swedes seem to consider Americans born dancers and Øke was shy. Jeannie finally just grabbed him, and the dancing went fine.

The Scandinavian countryside is not unlike the Fox Valley around Appleton, but because it is north European, and I first saw it at twentytwo, I observe it with a more kindly eye than I usually spare for Outagamie county. How snobbish I can be! In the Stockholm campground, reunited with *my* bus, I taught the students, at their request, a couple of Russian songs: "*Rassvetali yabloni i grushi.*" Peace or, at least, a truce. They had camped in a refuse dump on the way to Sweden and were filled with the very real triumph of having done everything wrong and survived.

I woke up between five and six when the sun hit me. I was on a rocky cliff above the fjord that morning; the sky was blue, the Swedish ships passing were clean and white, and Walt Drymalski, with whom I had argued and agreed and drunk beer until late into the night, had left his rod and reel beside my sleeping bag for me to use. I did. The rainbow trout are prismbright in that clear water.

Last evening we found a place on this cliff where there were enough pine needles to insert tent pegs and in that way managed to avoid the crowd in the main camp. Since it was a holiday night, almost Midsummer's Eve, too much beer was drunk by all, and a Swedish policeman together with an Alsatian police dog appeared about midnight to ask for quiet. The students, who had been talking, among other things, of revolution, immediately pointed to me. "Der Herr Professor Doktor Yatzeck." (I had taught them that as a joke, of course, but they were smart enough to use it.) I, who was mere minutes before a convicted representative of the "Fascist Establishment," was nevertheless expected to retrieve the situation. The policeman, very polite to a "Professor," happily watched the students disappear into their tents when I called out "Bed time!"

After a lethargic start, we had a good and short drive to the ferry at Nortalje. All six buses arrived, drove on the ferry, and fell into an all-night bull session, a good one. We met two Finns, one a Social Democrat, one a Communist, who knew, between them, some Russian, English, and German. With four of the students we talked politics and the possibility of loyalty to anything larger than one's home village 'til 3:00 a.m. Now and then, in that white night, we passed tiny islands, often sheltering a single cabin and a boat. They looked like the very essence of "home," selfcontained and selfsufficient, just the right size for loyalty. (That must have been between Åland and Turku.)

We nocturnal politicians slept through the arrival in Turku and the drive to the Finnish capital. Helsinki was still European, rather than Californian, and relatively shabby. Machinegun scars from the 1940 Winter War with the Russians were sharply visible. I noticed something I had not seen for a long time, and certainly not in contemporary Hamburg or Stockholm: the womanliness of a certain kind of European woman - often poorly dressed, but always with style - sexy, but not in the American, striven-for manner. These Finnish ladies were conscious of themselves, glad to be admired, but not bothering much about it. I don't know if I can explain this well. The main ingredient is not sex, but self-possession, not *trying* to be anything, and it conveys the electricity that Pasternak speaks of when describing Lara: beautiful in *herself.*

We met the Gypsies in Helsinki. They were on their way to an annual Gypsy summer gathering, though we never found out where. Gypsies are always on their way. We were, by contrast, utterly amateur voyagers and thus, from their point of view, helpless prey. One of our cohorts, Frank Schafer, somehow offended a Gypsy grandmother and brought down a curse on his van which was, unfortunately, also colleague George's van. There was, throughout the following six weeks of Russian roads, hardly a day when the "Gray Goose" didn't lose a windshield to Russian road gravel or simply wobbled to a helpless, unplanned halt. Flat tires were constant. We were often forced to divide the van's occupants and carry them on other vans while towing the helpless Goose. This meant that the Goose's inhabitants had to travel without their luggage or kitchen supplies, like peanut butter. We did, though glumly enough, share with them. Finally, the Goose was safely dragged to Kiev, where a thirsty master machinist spent a rainy Sunday morning turning a new piston for the price of a bottle of vodka. On this first cursed yet blessed trip, it also rained eighty-five days out of one hundred and I, thirty-six and still married, fell in love. (Frank Schafer, wherever he is, has much to answer for.)

To run far ahead of my tale for a moment, the new piston got us halfway to Odessa. We dragged the Goose empty the rest of the way and shipped her, with George and a full complement of students, to Istanbul and the nearest

VW garage. Our resident mechanic, having sold his passport, jumped aboard that same ship and hid. I don't know how he entered Turkey, but we were left without a repairman. All of this, all of it, Frank, because you stopped singing "Hey, Jude" just long enough to badmouth that Gypsy grandmother in Helsinki.

Further, befriended by cute, Gypsy children, our mellowest van lost its clothes, cash, and even an iron reserve of traveler's checks. Again, I personally dragged three Gypsy boys out of our van, and emptied their pockets of Walkmans and tapes, though I do hate Walkmans. I believe, finally, that the imploring Gypsy mothers at every Moscow stoplight were carrying large, *rented* babies. Our commerce, then, with Gypsies was, well, confrontational. Still, their bright clothing in a dreary world, the sound of their flutes and violins on damp Russian evenings, their supreme ability to live off the land; in sum, their ancient nomadic existence, like that of the Mongol-Tatars say, has also, like the fearsome attraction of wolves, a dangerous magnetism for something in my own nature. Bruce Chatwin quotes a Mongolian poem:

You have a house and a mill.

I have a horse and a whip.

I will kill you, and go.

I find these lines, at odd moments, weirdly attractive, in Russian, *zhutko khorosho.*

After Helsinki and its Gypsy grandmother, we rolled on to Hamina, the last Finnish town before the Soviet border. Hamina campground offers a rough, sprawling log sauna on the Gulf of Finland and the last chance to store away Western delicacies: hams, oranges, even toilet paper. After shopping and a sauna, we risked Ultimate Frisbee among very sharp, black rocks out in that Gulf.

There had been little advertising along the roads, the countryside not yet swinish with beer cans, and, among the Finns, an ironic and quiet view of socialism *and* capitalism. They killed the Russians five for one in 1940, on skis and with knives (*finnkas*), surrendered only when the Red Army took Helsinki, and were very much on their own side.

The Hamina town square was our rallying point for the invasion of Russia. Someone brought a cardboard marshal's baton for George, photographs were taken of the still neat platoon of VW buses, George shouted a John Wayne "Ho-o-o!" and off we charged. Steve, who had rather copiously celebrated his last night in freedom, dressed for this crucial border crossing by finally standing upright in his tent, thus ripping tent and wrenching out tent pegs, belting this outfit with the laundry line, including laundry, and then rolled back into the food storage shelf of our bus. Steve was the ultimate of cool: his Russian grammar was nonexistent and yet he became, nevertheless, one of the best of our speakers on the coming Russian roads, for his ears were good, as was his memory. Best of all, he could ignore, or didn't feel, the stress of new encounters.

***

"We are inclined to accept the spirit as readily as the flesh."

Andrey Sinyavsky, *A Voice from the Chorus*

***

Whatever real dangers may have been present, the actual crossing of the Soviet/Finnish border provoked an almost superstitious fear. This was, no doubt, due in part to the rhetoric of the Cold War, but the season played its part as well. We always crossed a day or two after the Scandinavian celebration of Midsummer's Day, the sky barely darkened at night, and our heads were full of Dostoevsky's *White Nights* and *Crime and Punishment*. Suburbanites all, we wanted the ominous, we wanted to be frightened. The Soviet border troops generally obliged.

Fifteen, or perhaps fifty kilometers out of Hamina, the physical distance isn't the point, on a gravel road surrounded by Finnish mist and spiky conifers, we passed gray-clad Finnish troops. Then, in a black-magical fifty yards, we spotted a khaki-clad Russian with a tommygun, a green band around his service cap, and a fierce-looking guard dog. This apparition checked the lead van's papers, raised the red-and-white painted wooden bar - like a railroad crossing barrier - saluted, and beckoned us past. We climbed, then, along rutted stone and clay to the top of a low, bald hill and pulled up beside a ramshackle wooden barracks with guard kiosks in front and a row of what looked like oil pits. These were for inspecting the undersides of vehicles. An officer and a couple of slovenly privates collected our passports, the papers for all of the vans, ordered us to get out and requested that we utterly unload. As traffic is light here, the border guards inspected every tent, sleeping bag, with a cold-eyed roughness just short of sadism. English language books sporting the hammer and sickle on the cover were confiscated. Those with the barber-pole cathedral of Vassily the Blessed or with beaming Russian grandmothers were given back. None of the guards seemed competent in English. The search procedure took four hours or so. Actually, we enjoyed it. We enjoyed our mild fix of Soviet brutality.

Our leader, George, having served in military intelligence, half expected to be turned back, expelled. He kissed the Tolstoyan earth when it appeared that the insidious, all-knowing Soviets didn't have a file on him. As a first installment of the Gypsy curse, George's bus had a flat tire right at the border. A short, stocky Russian civilian simply picked up the back corner of the loaded vehicle when we couldn't immediately find the jack to change the tire. He accepted no reward, and said "My pleasure, friends," and then evaporated.

There were several hairy moments. First, a guard with a hand-held metal detector picked up the knot of gold chain that I was smuggling in for friends. As precious metals are contraband, I could have been turned back, even arrested, but as I sweated a big drop, the guard simply said "loose change" and passed me without checking my pockets. Then, a Dutch couple applied to us for translation help. Driving a propane-fueled car with a large gas cylinder in the trunk, they hurriedly explained that the guards were about to penetrate this odd tank with a blowtorch to see what it contained. Our shouts of "PROPAN! PROPAN!" finally got through to the blowtorch operator and just averted an explosive border incident.

Finally, Wesley, the born-again wheeler-dealer, was attempting to slide through with a dozen Bibles. As the search of our bus intensified, it developed that he had also hidden a *Playboy* magazine under *my* seat, thinking it might be saleable but knowing it was forbidden, like the three pairs of jeans that he was wearing to peddle in Leningrad. (When I asked Wesley about born-again Christianity and greed, he explained that whatever made him happy also pleased Jesus.) In any event, the Bibles and the *Playboy* added a good hour to our halt at the border. The best of the adventure was the Solomonic judgment of the woman officer in charge of searching us. Her unusual neatness and dutiful air made us tremble. She was patently a very straight *komsomolka* in good Party standing. Still, she twinkled a bit as she pronounced:

"We take eleven Bible, and *Playboy*. You, Vesley, take one Bible. You need." There was also a good deal of bass giggling when the forbidden magazine unaccountably appeared in the guard kiosk, where the hams and sausages confiscated as carriers of foot and mouth disease were being consumed. Still, except for Wesley, we went our way, finally, rejoicing.

A bungled Bible shipment fits here because our student trip to Russia was in the nature of a pilgrimage. We were, of course, not on our way to the Holy Sepulcher, but to socialist "stations of the Cross," so to speak. Lacking, as Russian governments have always lacked, material benefits to shower upon a grateful people, Marxist ideology simply took the place of traditional religion here as the "opiate of the masses."

Beginning at the border, in Vyborg, Leningrad, Novgorod, and Moscow, seemingly every flat surface bore white-lettered red banners proclaiming that "Lenin lived, lives, will live," or that "Lenin is with us!" His relics in the red and black marble tomb in Red Square liken him to the Orthodox saints and monks on view in the Cave Monastery in Kiev. The omnipresent *znachky*, tiny lapel pins, portrayed Lenin, Stalin, and lesser notables of socialism in very much the manner of religious medals. As Sinyavsky wrote, Russians do "accept the spirit as readily as the flesh." They have never developed the habit of plenty. Wesley's Bibles would have fallen on fertile ground, and probably did, for the badly paid border guards most likely merchandized them. On the other hand, the young woman in charge may equally, and *religiously*, have burned them.

Beyond the border, there was nothing for fifty kilometers but a bad, sad road with conifers, and occasional kids shouting, begging "kau-gummi," the German for chewing gum. There was, indeed, until the later '80s, no road as good as an average Wisconsin two-lane, city boulevards excepted. Russians and their goods move, still, mostly by train. Only beyond Vyborg did we see towns and villages, and they reminded me of Walker Evans's photographs of the Depression South. Finland and the U.S. were in another century, except, say, for the Bronx. Which side am I on?

The students earnestly practiced Russian with the Intourist guide who joined us in Vyborg, when I had the sense to let them get a word in edgewise. The physical poverty of the country was so striking that they did not make comparisons. Although some guides had a certain stock set of propaganda speeches, one - Raya - more practically explained the necessity of making pit stops in the woods. Socialist toilets were really too much for green foreigners. Indeed, all public conveniences, trams, say, or elevators, were, and still are, messy, and tend to work more or less spasmodically, except for the Moscow subway, still *the* parade piece, far superior to London's neglected tube, still safer than New York's. This paragon, however, like the White Sea Canal, was mostly built with the labor of political prisoners in Stalin's time.

Just outside St. Petersburg, we found our motel, built for the Olympics, already visibly cracking and decomposing. Thrown up to meet a deadline, the cement was poured in zero degree weather. An all-night bar featured the latest pirated rock music and New York prices. The Russians who frequented it, reminiscent of the well-connected *stilyagi* of '61, were much better dressed than we were. They certainly didn't ask to buy our Levis. *They* wore designer jeans.

At 10:00 a.m. a Russian charwoman, one of the millions of such earnest *babushki,* was trying to get a literally stiff young man to bed before the officious doorman could have him hauled off to the "sobering up station." She was not his grandmother, but said, as I took his feet, and she his shoulders, that she was responsible for him. I asked why. She said, "For Christ's sake," with the intonation of an answer, not an exclamation. Russia is Dostoevsky country still.

Later that same day, we visited an Orthodox service, and another *babushka* approached me to ask that I "organize" monetary help for a blind woman seated at the entrance. Embarrassed, I had to admit that neither I, nor my students, had been able to exchange money yet. "It doesn't matter, *nichevo,* said the woman, so bent herself with arthritis that she was forced to look along a raised shoulder to regard me from below. "Just pat her a bit, then." For Christ's sake, I guessed. I wanted to be on that woman's side, but I found it hard to "pat" her protégée. I was, I guess, far too Anglo-Saxon, but I had been given a piece of the Russian puzzle.

The week in Leningrad did not continue this well. The Intourist guides insisted on World War II memorials and all-day tours of the city. This kept us grouped as "the Americans" and denied us conversation with old Russians sitting in parks. Leslie, the vegetarian girl, refused to continue a discussion about Shakespeare at lunch because her peers would find this pretentious. The vegetarian boy, Eric, and I hunted for an ice cream cone, following a trail of happy lickers, but the ice cream cart, when we found it, was sold out.

However, as evening arrived, Ann, the artist, had met a couple of sailors upon whom to sharpen her Russian (and they *were* handsome sailors) leaning against the edge of a fountain from the time of Catherine. Later, we made it into "Sadko," a restaurant with the motif of a Novgorodian folk tale, where a quiet, preppy-looking Russian interrupted our efforts at square dancing to the balalaika to teach us, quite without words, a slow, elegant circle dance. It's the kind that the "Beryozka" troupe does at Carnegie Hall, which gives the impression that the dancers are all on tiny, brass wheels. The evening was good - indeed, the reverse of the Russian proverb - for it was "wiser than morning."

The first stage of our Russian experience always involved a war with Intourist. The guides assigned us were supposed to keep us grouped and to fill our days with what they seemed to consider progress and we saw as propaganda. Our innate chaos rather quickly wore down the guides. As soon as we were away from their home turf, generally Leningrad or Moscow, they "waved their hands," *makhnuli rukami*, at our lack of order, and let their own native anarchism relish what their socialist discipline could not control. This was both good and bad. We were free to do as we liked, but we missed real Russian treasures: a fine museum of the Kursk Bulge, the beginning of the ultimate Soviet counter-offensive against the Germans, or the painter Repin's dacha near Leningrad, because the guides soon began to think that we would never be interested or punctual. Without a fixed class schedule and with repeated disappointments, as when once Tolstoy's estata, Yasnaya Polyana, was inexplicably closed for repairs, the students devoted themselves to bare physical survival: more sleep, or keeping out of the heat or rain, and found it hard to be "up" for a monastery or a monument. There was always, near the surface, the feeling that monasteries and monuments were academic, i.e., not real. Still, the problem was a mixture of American attitudes and Russian difficulties. Isn't that exactly the problem with any diplomacy?

Leningrad, christened St. Petersburg, has also been called Petrograd, when the German *burg* was too reminiscent of the Teutonic enemy. The city was renamed Leningrad when Lenin assumed Peter's mantle. The inhabitants, indifferent to or, perhaps, flouting high politics, generally call their town "Peter," far from politically feverish Moscow, which became the capital again under Lenin and the Soviets, the citizens have tended to be an independent lot. It was no accident that Stalin had Kirov, the Leningrad Party Secretary, murdered, and then began the terrible purges of the thirties from this spot. In 1961, after a revaluation of the ruble, I read the following on a sign affixed to an old woman's newspaper kiosk: "We neither understand nor accept the new money." In 1990, with most of the taxi drivers charging foreigners ten dollars and a pack of Marlboros for any ride, at least one old socialist we met charged the usual price in rubles - about a dollar - for the same ride. Then, finding us to be Americans, stopped to buy us a doll in peasant dress as a souvenir. Cantankerous folks, and willing to lose by it!

Why do I come here? For the melodious phrase of an old woman at the well near the artist Repin's dacha: *"khoroshaya voditsa,"* "good water," or the latest slang: *"On ni boom-boom,"* "He hasn't a clue." For the generosity of Raya and Boris who share their boiled potatoes, wisely prepared in advance, with us when we run out of bread. For the glimmers of recognition among the students when they first see "The Bronze Horseman" and remember Pushkin's poem. For the moments when I can be as feckless as they seem and delight in a ridiculous sign beside the road to Leningrad: *"Berigitye muravyei!,"* "Preserve the ants!" Boris, grinning, explained that this was not a cheerful Soviet acceptance of Dostoevsky's definition of socialism as an anthill. It was, rather, the mark of a budding interest in ecology, for ants aerate the soil.

Whatever its official title, this "northern Palmyra" continues to strike the classical note of that Middle Eastern namesake. For me, the city's heart is the Winter Palace on Palace Square, which, with its wing the Hermitage, houses Russia's largest collection of Western art.

Rembrandt, for instance, can almost be measured by the acre. Like the city's original suffix "burg," the largely Italianate official architecture, and the Venetian canals, the museum is an example of Russia's Western face, of the excruciating and often bitterly divisive attempt to be European. Of course, this was Peter's intention, for he felt that Russia could survive only on European terms. Still, even this massive monument to Western genius harbors the contradictions of Peter's reforms.

These contradictions became apparent as soon as we arrived, tickets in hand, at the edge of Palace Square, the imperial setting of the Hermitage. The palace, with the square behind it, built directly on the Neva River, is pure eighteenth century in form, but both palace and square are so vast that they echo, almost, the steppes. One remembers that Peter was seven feet tall, and the empire came to cover a sixth of the earth's land surface. Alexander the First's column in the center of the square, built to commemorate the victory over Napoleon, inspires, since Pushkin, subversive thoughts:

I raised myself a monument not made by hands.

Higher than Alexander's column it proudly stands.

That is, the inspired poet, like the icon painter, fulfills the work of the spirit: "a monument not made by hands." An imitative classical column surmounted by a tsar, no matter how sumptuous, cannot really compete.

Within, as without, the very size of the Winter Palace weighs European forms against Russian vastness. Acres of marble stairway, tons of green-gleaming malachite from the Urals testify to the size of even the westernized Russian's dreams and imagination. One could not, for a moment, confuse this structure with the Louvre, though its content certainly rivals that of the Parisian cynosure. Russian in size, it is also Russian-dingy, Russian-crowded, unventilated, and wretchedly lit. I recognize the Russian habit of ignoring most merely physical discomforts. Infected, though not, I think, terminally, with the contemporary craze for Impressionism, a friend and I abandoned the group tour to specialize in Monet and Matisse. Three large second-floor halls harbor a fine collection of these artists' works. Framed in glass, which reflected the lovely gray light of the square below, Waterloo Bridge, and even the more than famous water lilies of Giverny, were essentially invisible. Being Western, we cursed the conditions, despaired. Right then, however, a *babushka,* a museum guard in this case, set to watch over the Monets, took pity on us. Indeed, that seems to be the primary function of these omnipresent benign spirits. She rose from her knitting and seized us, in turn. Gravely pacing, she placed us on just that square of neglected oak parquet from which the foggy Thames, the gleaming lily-ponds, could be best admired. The execrable glass and its reflections disappeared. We were in Monet's London, in provincial France, and then in paradise with Matisse's dancers. When she found that we could, in a manner, speak Russian, this most admirable woman explained that the museum offers free seminars to those of its guards who wish to attend, that she had come to know at least the most prominent beauties of the collection and where to stand to view them. This work, which she loved, makes her tiny pension almost livable. For her, as ultimately for us, this Hermitage, wretchedly crowded and lit, is the temple of art that Catherine the Great envisaged.

In this most European structure, Russian impossibilities had been hardily and neatly surmounted, though not at all removed. My example will seem frivolous, but it is in just this manner, the investment of that patience and ingenuity which define love, that these people, these women in particular, contrive to endure.

Afterwards, in the Palace Square, it occurred to me that the perfect finale to such an experience would be a dish of Russian ice cream, which can rival the Italian, and a glass of Russian champagne. Once, in 1961, such delicacies had been available at the foot of Nevsky Prospect, the main street, and just two blocks from where we stood. Would the champagne and ice cream shop today, as is so often the case in Russia, be closed, under reconstruction, doing inventory, or simply dark? Depending now on serendipity, which is, strictly speaking, impossible, I led the way to the foot of Nevsky. The shop was open, uncrowded, and offered the desired delicacies. Our toasts, to the museum *babushka,* to Russia's survival, to synchronicity, were heartfelt.

Our city tours here have tended, of course, to be largely aesthetic, given the presence of the Hermitage and the fine, though lesser known, Russian Museum of native works. Indeed, the city itself has a special, perhaps brutally aesthetic quality, because it was so obviously willed. Built by Peter's order, and with slave labor, in a malarial swamp, on driven tree trunks, there are many human bones at its root. The layout is as geometric as possible given the numerous islands. Catherine the Great's monument to Peter, Falconet's "Bronze Horseman," is the theoretical center of this geometry. That statue, which Pushkin took as the title of his most seminal work, embodies, as Pushkin suggests, the ruthless, and some think necessary, desire to succeed that is, for Russians, the Western element. The Neva flows before the "Horseman," the lovely, granite-lined canals run concentrically behind it. St. Petersburg is, indeed, "a window hacked into Europe" for trade and for naval supremacy on the Baltic. However, like London, Hamburg, or any port city, the sea wind brings freedom to breathe and to think that the hinterland doesn't always know.

Our students loved the atmosphere of the "white nights" when, unable to sleep, we prowled the wide Nevsky Prospect, the Winter Palace Square, and admired the hugely delicate violets and sunflowers of the old cast iron fences: a city trademark. As Pushkin testified, one *can* read the newspaper at midnight without a lamp during that summer season. However, not being political sorts, we tended to complain at the absence of baseball scores rather than cheer for the opening of new hydro-electric stations.

Sometimes, on the Finnish Gulf, we built campfires on the beach, swam in the milky night waters, and talked. Once a young-old woman, and Russian life ages women quickly, remembered the nine hundred days of the German encirclement during World War II. Constant shelling, though the Finns, in their tepid alliance with the Germans, mostly fired high, aware that they would have to live with Russian neighbors after the conflict. The inhabitants knew bitter cold and wracking hunger, for it proved impossible to sufficiently supply the city across the ice of Lake Ladoga. The "Fascists" - the term always used by Russians for the German enemy of that time - never took the city. Our guest, who had been drinking, an unusual thing for Russian women, described the surreptitious burial of her starved children. She buried three, one after another, at night "so that they would not be eaten." This left us, for once, quite silent.

On another occasion, one of the overseers of the camp praised her government pension, a commonplace under Soviet rule. Yes, she knew of Stalin's abuses and crimes. Who hadn't lost relatives and friends in the purges? Still, she took what now seems, to me, a typically Russian view of the matter: *"They* have always overworked, starved, and murdered us. The miracle is that now so many have a crust of bread and can die *their own deaths."* This is the Russian expression for dying in one's own bed and of natural causes. "That's luxury for you!" she added. Her words were utterly innocent of irony. Appleton, Wisconsin, seemed very far away.

In the environs of St. Petersburg, we usually visited Peterhof, the Founder's summer palace on the Gulf, tsarskoe Selo, Catherine's summer home and Pavlovsk, her son Paul's country place. The heavily gilded fountains in the shapes of the gods and monsters of Greek myth, the ordered parks and ornate, rococo halls of all three, the acres of gold leaf, the classically geometric layouts, indicate how very Western this dynasty strove to be. The long grass insistently invading the formal grounds and the holes in the ceilings left by German and Russian target practice in WWII, suggested clearly that Western order does not maintain itself.

In any event, I soon reached my quota of such order and took refuge by rosy, lichen covered brick walls and battered gates where buskers, now deprived of their former state scholarships, raise well-worn French horns and cornets to celebrate Corelli and Gabrieli. When sighting American tourists, they even play "Home on the Range" and, not surprisingly, "Joe Hill," the famous labor union song. The music somehow fits, glitters even, but warms in a way that gold leaf doesn't. Still, I'm happy when we're on the road to Novgorod.

This is oldest Russia, *Rus'* to initiates. The Novgorod Kremlin, for "kremlin" means simply "city stronghold" and was a feature of many old Russian towns, contains St. Sophia, the cathedral modeled upon that in Kiev. Both attempt to mirror the Orthodox mother church in Constantinople. Here also is the Great Bell, once used to call the city council or *veshch* into session, for Novgorod was the seat of a representative merchant polity before being conquered by Ivan the Terrible. The Great Bell is tongueless, martyred for having frightened a visiting tsar's horse, or so the story goes. Novgorod had been a Hansa center, a trading post of that great international mercantile order of the Baltic, long after being founded by Viking merchants.

Sophia, the Church of the Holy Wisdom, has great bronze doors cast in Magdeburg with wide-mouthed lion door handles and Biblical scenes in which the bulging eyes of the figures are reminiscent of the chess figures carved of walrus ivory by those same Vikings. Russia was, indeed, before the Tatar yoke, variously and closely connected with northern Europe. Within the church, however, the gifts of Ivan the Terrible, a great silver chandelier, an ornate tsar's box-throne where he, on visits, sat alone while all else stood in prayer, attest to Moscow's ultimate dominance.

Above, in the limestone gallery, there is a telling collection of graffiti incised by other earlier worshippers in the twelfth century:

"May your hands wither, oh sinful soul."

"Noblemen's dishonor."

"And I cry out: Oh my soul, why do you lie in luxury, why do you not rise up, why do you not adore your Lord? Why do you thirst for good, neglecting to do good?"

Below these, and my favorite, is an odd little spell: "Pies in the oven, mushrooms in the dish, a quail rises in the oak grove. Serve the boiled groats, serve the pies. Go there." I certainly will.

In the sanctuary below are incense and chanting and the mild glances of the icons. No, the St. Petersburg palaces of the eighteenth-century monarchs are not essential Russia. This view is fortified by at least a dozen small stone churches, each the gift of an ancient merchant family, which line the Volkhov River that splits Novgorod, some of them graced with the fiercer, hauntingly judgmental icons of Feofan Grek. Best of all is the outdoor museum of wooden architecture across from the town. Fir peasant huts, mills, barns, and churches were numbered and taken down in their native villages and brought here to celebrate the pine art of the north. Artisans - spinners, weavers and woodcarvers - can be seen at their trades, shabbier and more believable than at Williamsburg, impressive in the pride they bring to the task. The horse head ends of roof beams, incised suns and moons, attest to a pagan, Scandinavian ambience here. Intricate, lacy window frames display the ability of carpenters working largely with stone-honed hatchets rather than scroll saws. As no one now lives in these handsome structures, swallows nest in the many cracks and apertures and fill the air, the day, with purposeful, mosquito-fed twittering. Like these birds, the north Russians used the material of the region to build and survive. Unlike them, they spared some effort to include beauty shaved and hacked from close-grained spruce. There is hope in this. Humans need beauty.

The road from Novgorod to Moscow is little repaired though much used. Whoever was driving the van had to keep his eyes on the rutted macadam. The navigator clutched a rather too schematic map. (Complaining of this to the Intourist guide, I was answered: "If you don't know where you're going, you'd probably better not go there.") The rest of us saw what seemed to be one village, or many villages run into one. In earlier times, goings and comings of tourists were very closely watched. Later, we simply got lost, and this could be quite enjoyable. Usually, however, we kept to the main road, admired the lovely and various window frames - not museum pieces only - and marveled at the small size of old and new log cabins. (In areas of historical preservation, if one does build, one is required to build a log cabin.) The homes are not much larger than single garages in the States. This does make them easier to heat with wood stoves, however. Here, too, on new structures, suns, stars, horse's heads, and abstract curlicues encircle small, dark panes.

Our last stop before Moscow was Klin, Tchaikovsky's hometown. The Tchaikovsky house/museum is a sprawling, gray clapboard structure with many decorated porches. "The 1812 Overture" resounds in the large, macadam parking lot. At this museum, Tchaikovsky's music, the whole *oeuvre*, is played constantly during working hours. In a separate auditorium, one may choose a favorite work. We secured tickets, were assigned a guide, and accomplished a pious tour of rooms full of Victoriana: fringed lamps and tablecloths, oil portraits of the composer, his friends and family, and a grand piano in almost every room, usually a Bechstein. We walked the highly polished floors in felt over-slippers, as in all such museums, and deposited them in a huge wooden crate, which was, at intervals, exchanged for its empty twin in the foyer. The guide's patter resembled hagiography and was certainly not contemporary psychobiography. I find this rather pleasing and enjoy the strains of *Swan Lake*. Why *shouldn't* the great artists be saints? Still, the best part of this visit, for me, was the large, grass-grown yard full of great old trees. Here, our own Intourist guide strolled and recited *Eugene Onegin* by heart, as in a play of Chekhov, and was charmingly melancholy. She was not unusual in her expertise. I have met naval engineers touring the States who knew Pushkin just as well. As Raya recited, her great pride in Russia's culture was warmly evident.

I knew from earlier conversations that Raya accompanied western visitors who could only pity or sneer while viewing her country. The students, quite aware of this psychological electricity, were more than properly respectful, as when visiting a church in which one doesn't know the rite. They didn't even laugh when the needle stuck at "*1812's*" cannons. I was proud of them. Somehow, they learned there is no need to ridicule the foreign, so we progressed thoughtfully toward Moscow with Napoleon's cannon ringing forty-three times in our ears.

Our next stop *was* Moscow, and a fine old town it is, but I am no townsman. Summers, when I was not with the students in Eastern Europe, I spent those months cutting hay for my friend and neighbor Dennis. It is his opinion that a professor may be trusted to work on a farm if given a single chore, like cutting hay, and a few years, twelve in my case, to learn the ropes. I missed the summer alfalfa fields when in Russia, and kept an eye out for agricultural matters to report to Dennis. Just then, though, what struck me was the particular soft orange-red of field poppies in young rye, found from Belgium to Russia and, of course, reminiscent of the blood shed in Europe's great suicidal wars. Then there was the patient flow of sheep around the van when we met a flock in a narrow lane. They were weighty, cinnamon brown, and undulating like a woolly river. Other times we met the more threatening shoving of big, dark cream, horned cattle. Always following these herds was a thin, ragged herder with his scruffy, black-and-white, right hand, his dog. I imagined then his summer life as something a good deal nearer the real elements, rain and sun and hard stone, than our cushioned riding. Still, we shared the same long, rutted road, the three months of the same soft season.

CHAPTER III
Moscow

The first morning in a new city was always spent on a quick orientation tour before loosing the students on the town. Lucia, the Moscow guide riding in my bus, spoke slowly enough that the students and I, still rusty, could understand. We got a quick initial ride around Red Square, Gorky Street, for bookstores, and then drove south to the New Virgin Monastery. The "celebrity" cemetery there contained the graves of Gogol, Chekhov, and Stalin's wife. All of the plots were well tended, covered with fresh flowers, radiating heat in the hush before a rainstorm. This red brick fort, enclosing a fine sixteenth century bell tower and the deep blue, starred onion domes of the monastery church, guards only the dead now, but it served earlier as a prison. When the older sister of Peter the Great, Sophia, tried to seize power from the monastery cell to which she had been relegated, the authorities changed the locks, and she became a close-kept prisoner. Indeed, divorce being practically impossible, it was a habit of rulers like Ivan the Terrible to encourage unfruitful wives to take the veil in these fortress-like monasteries. In such cases, with the Orthodox Metropolitan's permission, a new marriage could be arranged.

As we were returning through Manezh Square, Raya, our regular trip guide who, I realized too late, didn't know how to drive, told me to cross three lanes of traffic to make a useful but illegal right turn. I complied, assuming that she knew what she was doing, but was whistled to a stop by a militiaman on his high traffic control perch. Wondering if jail were anything like the New Virgin Monastery, I pretended ignorance of Russian. The militiaman rightly called me a homicidal maniac, and then he allowed us to leave with a warning and the remark, right in my face, "Let him drive as he likes at home. Here he must follow the rules!"

Dinner at the restaurant *"Slavyansky Bazaar:"* fish soup and beef and potatoes, with Tsinandali, a Georgian white wine, extinguished the sting of the militiaman's remarks. After the usually rather sketchy bus cooking, there was a tremendous primitive satisfaction in a warmly filled belly. We returned then to the Mozhaisk campground along the road that Pierre follows in *War and Peace* as he rushes to the battle of Borodino.

A refreshing snooze in my tent was interrupted by Jeannie who was, she said, unable to drive off a lovesick Ukrainian. When I tried to send him packing, good old Jeannie winked and waved at him over my shoulder. I gave up, then, and rolled back into my sleeping bag. Who needs to be a white knight? Let her sort it out herself! Kids! Or, maybe, people!

The following day, scheduled for free exploration, some of us visited Pasternak's grave at Peredelkino. A plain wedge of white stone and that profile: an Arab stallion, the grave was one azure mass of forget-me-nots under three great pines, a good place. Then, as we did not like the idea of "touring" the small Peredelkino church during a service, we played "listening

Tom" on the small, lovely stone porch of the building and heard the rich roar of a Russian seven-fold "Amen" while tracing, with a delicate finger, the features of a limestone demon. No harsh fate. After the service I was able to buy a small paper icon of Sergey of Radonezh, *the* north Russian saint, founder of the *lavra* or great monastery at Zagorsk.

This pilgrimage to Pasternak's grave at Peredelkino had the further result that a priest, after the church service, guided us to the church of the Old Believers in Moscow. Before we left Peredelkino though, Margaret found a corner with daisies - *margaritky,* wild cornflowers - *vasilky,* volunteer rusty-red marigolds, a variety of orchid and a blue, trumpet-shaped hollyhock. Such simple things warmed the day. When we got to the church of the Old Believers there was a funeral in progress. Fearsome old women anathematized us, but then a deacon took pity and showed us the very oldest icons. Our priest-guide inscribed a book of reproductions of these treasures as a gift for "the Americans." This seemed worth the anathemas.

The next Moscow day was dedicated to shopping, the primary American sport. Friend Walt, just an average Russian student but a secular saint, asked me to help him find Havana cigars. I was glad to oblige.

This Walt was a useful type to know: practical, able, handy with automobile motors, and yet both *schlemiel* and *schlimazel* at once. Like me, he was liable at any moment to drop the frothing chicken soup into his own quivering lap. We were twins that way. When I first knew him, he was a natural, i.e., unideological, hippy, born with that Chekhov moustache, planning to be a "lifer" or five-year student at Lawrence, crown prince and heir of the Polonia Coal Company in south Chicago. I swear that he majored in Russian because he could curse in Polish and thought that would be sufficient. Those few Polish monosyllables were almost the whole treasure of the linguistic island that Walt inhabited. Yet, he was people-shrewd, and could turn on you, too.

On July Fourth in Moscow, Walt and I were shopping together for Havana cigars, but also because we were supposed to cook the evening meal for our bus mates. Walt knew that my shy demeanor would get him the cigars and even Soviet champagne faster than his 73rd Street Polish would. (He had very nearly burned down the humanities building at the college by pitching a cigar in the classroom wastebasket.) I miss him.

After we hunted out the Beryozka dollar shop in Gorky Street and bought bubbly and cigars, we were stopped - "Hey, Ami!" - right there on the main drag by a Russian punk who wanted to buy my Levis. He said, rightly, that I was too old and too fat to wear jeans anyway. Though long out of teenaged Marxism, I still didn't like to sell things. I gave the greasy-eyed punk Lecture B on the anti-social nature of the black market.

The punk said: "For a Russian professor you speak lousy Russian. Where did you learn it, in Zambia?"

My Polish prince, catching the gist, lost control. He had to sit on the saliva-stained curb to finish laughing. I would have dropped the "F" bomb on the punk if I'd known the Russian words. Wordless, I just stood stupidly, like somebody's ox that doesn't yet know it's been pole-axed. The punk spit, profoundly, and took off. Walt rose, swinging his Beryozka bag, not dreaming of commiseration. How often had I told *him* that he was, at most, a Kennedy or "gentleman's C" type Russian student?

Here, however, as never in Dostoevsky, the gods spoke. The badly glued bottom of Walt's shopping bag unfolded, three heavy green bottles struck the curb like Katyusha rockets, and we were bathed in sweet, sticky *shampanskoye*. It was worth the mess to see divine justice so quickly delivered, that one time in thirty-six years.

The wet and cleansing river Don was still to come, some thousand miles from Gorky Street and a week away, at least. We were fly bait on a steaming Moscow curb. I didn't point out the rightness of what had occurred, but suggested that we had just time for a sauna. Alexander Lipson, of sacred memory, had lectured the previous week in Boston on the Sandunov Baths. They were supposed to be behind the Hotel Berlin, downhill from the Lubyanka prison, but a fiercely steaming, utterly cleansing, *good* Hell. We sought, and as is seldom the case in Russian regions, we found.

There was, that July day, and maybe still is, a small, triangular, dusty park behind the Hotel Berlin in Moscow. In the park stood three dusty Lombardy poplars - called "American" poplars in Russia - and a dusty militiaman, or policeman, in blue and red. He wore white gloves which meant that he mustn't "touch" a suspect. (The ones who grab you are said to come in rusty raincoats, and at night.) This militiaman was lecturing a woman who was holding a urinating two-year-old over a small flowerbed. He was explaining about proper Soviet cleanliness and order. I translated for Walt, hoping to expunge the punk's judgment. "As well he may," said Walt. "As well I might have figured out for myself, even without the subjunctive." Having finished his speech, the militiaman saluted the two champagne-reeking foreigners (our shoes always gave us away.) Then the cop directed us to the fourth person in the little park, an old woman in black who was selling soap and birch branches. I had not asked the way to the baths. The militiaman was clairvoyant.

We bought soap that felt like pumice. The birch boughs were *venniky*, used at the baths to improve circulation, speed perspiration and impart a forest freshness, like *"Brut"* maybe. That is, you bludgeon one another with them. We bought these *venniky*, carried them across the street in the manner of Easter palms, and entered the Russian neoclassical portico that was revealed just behind the militiaman, the grandmother, and the carnations freshly sprinkled by the two-year-old.

A tawny and gray man, his face squeezed, as if in a vice, so that one eye was a good half inch higher than the other and almost invisible, was renting what looked like big, fuzzy towels. With my Zambian Russian, as good young Walt said, I found out the rules of play:

1) Clothes to be hung on rusty railroad spikes in the entry hall, a cavernous gym built of dirty-gray oolite, like a bank facade in Ohio.

2) Hot shower under the broken rubber hoses presumably inherited from the KGB neighbor just up the hill. (We decided to wear our reeking clothing for this part of the ceremony, and then let it drip dry.)

3) Three bastings in a steam chamber like the furnace room of the battleship Potyemkin. This cave was decorated with hanging gardens of

soot, wooden station benches, and a staircase to a high dais where beech chunks, the kiln-like furnace, and tough old men who could stand naked flame lived.

4) Three cooling plunges in a pond something like Helicon to alternate with the three bastings.

5) Bribe Cyclops and withdraw, as able.

Naked in the furnace room after our clothed shower, Walt and I witnessed the laser tongue of heat and flame emitted when the furnace was fed. Being fools, we hopped right up those stairs, took one shot of laser heat, retreated to the lower railroad bench area, and beat each other for stupidity with the now utterly desiccated birch boughs. Walt, feeling no doubt that the champagne justice inflicted by the Slavic god Perun had been a tad harsh, evened the score by pounding me until I was purple in unmentionable areas. Covered, like Siegfried, with birch leaves, the waters of life would have left more than a spot on my back untouched. I looked, felt, and smelled like the forest floor in November.

Next, the cooling pool: blue and gold tiled, circled by eight-foot golden figures of Roman gods, Mercury, Venus, Juno, and a figure that looked suspiciously like Stalin but was said to be Jupiter. We rolled, both aching - I *had* hit back - sweating into that cool blue. Birch leaves littered the agitated surface. Life returned. We could always, maybe, buy more champagne. We frolicked, but then it was over.

Bath custom absolutely demanded three parboilings near that laser-stove tended by those ancient Slavs and three dips amidst the Roman pantheon.

As we persevered, the heat got more bearable, the dips in the god-blessed pool more ethereal. We stayed the course, though our *venniky* were compost at the end. Walt seemed to feel that the scales of justice swung even again, when I finally allowed myself a tiny grimace under his woody chastisement.

After the third Hell, the third dip in the blue pool, we wrapped up in the towels - which were more like fuzzy sheets - and plopped down for a breather under the pair of signs in the Cyclops' den which commanded "NO SMOKING" and "NO DRINKING." Our tawny-gray host slip-slopped up to us across the unspeakably greasy stone floor with two bottles of Russian *"Zhigulovskoe"* beer in each hand, a cardboard package of "Belomorskii Kanal" cigarettes pinched under his crooked chin, and wooden matches behind his ears. He looked expectant. We satisfied him, i.e., I looked the other way, while Walt slipped him a fiver. When invited, Cyclops happily lit one of the Cuban lovelies that Walt retrieved from his knapsack. The cigar was champagne damp, but its sweet gurgling was as sensuous as Scriabin. I cherished my first really cold beer in two weeks in Europe; our host kept them at the bottom of that deep blue pool.

Then we talked. Now, since the meltdown of Soviet power in 1991, Russians talk as thirsty men drink. Then, 1969, was still a fairly lean time for conversation with real, that is, publicly unideological Russians. Cyclops, his off-square face and head seeming more and more normal, as the foamless, but feral Zhigulovskoe seeped and bubbled, told his Karamazovian life story. He interrupted himself only to supply - after the flames of Hell - other violators with other bottles and to pocket their remittances.

He had been born in Kharkov. He had fought at the Kursk Bulge or *duga*, where, as Churchill nicely put it, the Russians began the evisceration of the *Wehrmacht*. "My head squashed by *Panzer*," he said, "but also between two foreign elephants, Adam Smit (sic) and Karl Marx." We guessed that his *brains* hadn't been squashed.

Again, he claimed that he had finally left Kharkov not to escape the collective farm, but his wife who, as he put it, "sawed at him with a wooden saw," nagging slowly, leaving splinters. He went on at some length about the glories of Soviet agriculture. The corn on his collective farm had grown "all the way up to God." I asked whether he believed in God, and he said,"as much as I do in that corn." That had to suffice; that was the sum of Cyclops's theology.

After enough beer and Castro-leaf (though what, indeed, is enough?), Walt and I remembered that it was our turn to cook at the campground. We still needed to replace the champagne, but here, it turned out, our host could help us again, from the bottom of the pool, for another fiver. Then it really was time to leave.

When we had dressed in our rumpled best, our host came out on the porch of the baths with us and said farewell beside the lovely classical cement columns. We shook hands. He bowed and turned back to his den, to his work. Suddenly he stopped, drew his own wooly sheet around him like a toga, and declaimed: "Your side bugged our talk, our side bugged our talk, and fuck 'em both!" Walt and I droned "Amen!" It wasn't a verb that occurs in Dostoevsky, but it *was* the one I'd needed for that punk outside the *Beryozka*.

The next day, when we were scheduled to see the Kremlin, it turned out that the Kremlin was closed for cleaning, a "sanitary day." Our regular guide, Raya, suggested a trip out of Moscow to Zagorsk, to the one functioning Orthodox seminary in the Union and the next thing to Kremlin architecture. We were glad for any substitution and hoped to see the Kremlin churches on the next day.

When we crossed into the Soviet Union from Finland, we came from a pagan Midsummer's Night to daily socialist hagiography. This Leninist religion was practiced amid the many stone memories of Russian Orthodoxy. In Leningrad, the Museum of Atheism: icons with rubber tear ducts and red ink for blood was housed in the sweeping pillared half-circle which is the Kazan Cathedral. The church "On the Blood," dedicated to the memory of the assassinated tsar Alexander II, also rises in onion-domed glory in the center of that flat city of canals, and the neoclassical St. Isaac's, then a demonstration place for the workings of a huge pendulum, dominates downtown Leningrad much as the Capitol does Washington, D.C. No matter how scientific, rational, or materialistic the claims of Marxism were in Russia, it lived as a surrogate Orthodoxy. When our students developed their Kodak film, eighty percent of their pictures faithfully reflected the monuments of a thousand years of Orthodox Christianity that fill the Russian landscape. Finally, since one can only lose, materially speaking, by the practice of Christianity in the Soviet Union, it may well be argued that a majority of the world's genuine Christians live exactly there.

That our pilgrimage passed through a Holy Russia even under the

Soviet regime is not just a matter of *Marxist* hagiography, architecture, or Russian Christian poverty. The Orthodox Church itself survived. Our unexpected visit to Zagorsk suggested that Orthodoxy even flourished, at times. *Babushky,* those eternal Russian women in black who look seventy but are usually between thirty-five and fifty, regularly undertake fifty-mile pilgrimages on foot to obtain the intercession of the saint for some special intention. The place remained, then, this *Lavra* or Great Monastery of St. Sergius of Radonezh, a spiritual center of Russia even in the Soviet era. It witnessed to the spiritual limits restraining a most ruthless authoritarian state.

The deep blue, gold-starred domes, the "Trinity" of Rublyov, most Russian of icons, and the crowds of old and younger women with a sprinkling of men, amazed us and our cold-war-oriented students. Many in this crowd carried bottles, even teapots, in which to take home holy water.

However, there was another, most serendipitous attraction on this day. We accidentally hit upon the first visit of a foreign Orthodox dignitary since the Revolution. The Orthodox Metropolitan of Alexandria had come to Zagorsk to celebrate mass in the cathedral where the "Trinity" icon hangs. Bells tolled in every conceivable musical register. A strapping battalion of seminarians, black, blonde, and red beards streaming in the sonorous air, bellowed forth those unbelievably low notes for which the Russian liturgy is famous. Hosts of believers bent like wheat in the wind, sang with the young priests-to-be, and rejoiced in their reaffirmed faith. It is an oddity of Russians that the presence of guests, or of enemies, as in the case of the

Wehrmacht, brings out their faith in themselves, their true, generous powers. One furrowed *babushka* rushed up to a smoking student, Charlie, tore the Marlboro from his frozen lips, and shook an admonishing finger. This is holy ground. Smoking, "that which comes out of thy mouth," is an occasion of sin. Our guides, as always the purest young Soviets, fearing for us and for themselves, expected the frenzies of a religious riot.

No such thing occurred. We were guests.

We had, coming to Zagorsk, crossed another border. This border was more complex than the physical one between pagan Finland and the atheist Union. Here, thirty-three miles from Moscow, we felt again how Russia was torn, not between scientific Socialism and mystical Orthodoxy, but between two equally unworldly faiths. The nation, as opposed to the Party bosses, was materially poor, as always. It had suffered deprivation for the sake of a still unrealized Communist future not much differently than it suffered the thousand years of Orthodoxy which were, some churchmen thought, to make of Moscow a third and final Rome. The Moscow/Zagorsk border separated, really, two kinds of faith. Sixty-three years of Socialism had not radically altered Russian consciousness. It had merely, it seemed, changed the religious vocabulary. "Lenin Lives" is "Christ is Risen" is "I Work for a Jewish Carpenter" on the back of a Wisconsin Pentecostal's pickup truck.

On the next Moscow day, the Kremlin was still, inexplicably unavailable for visitation, I decided to find my Baptist friends of 1961, Olga and Sergey. I'd forgotten the address of the church. In the utter absence of city maps and telephone directories, I hired a taxi and said "take us to the Baptists."

The driver dropped me and three students, all unaware, at a synagogue. To Russians, apparently, all of these "sectarians" were the same. However, it turned out that the Baptist church was not far off, a series of *babushky* passed us from hand to hand, and when I knocked at the nondescript brick tenement, a young woman, nine years older than when I first came to this apartment building, which harbors the Baptist sanctuary, recognized me as "her first foreigner." She led us to Sergey's office. He was now editor of the Baptist *Brotherly Herald*, to which he gave me a subscription on the spot. He did translations from German in his church work, preached, sang in the choir, and quoted worldly passages from Lermontov. We were "of course" invited to share borscht and *kompot*, fruit marinated in fruit juice, with the church staff, then to attend an evening baptism and communion service.

Twenty-six adults were, one at a time, totally immersed in a pool that opened before the lectern. They were dressed in white sheets, athletically handled, and, sometimes, subdued by the very muscular senior minister. Sergey then preached very well on the motto set in stained glass in the window above the lectern: "God is Love" - *Bog est' Lyubov.'* Finally, my friend presided over an unusually substantial communion service. White-shirted deacons tore crusty chunks from three-pound loaves and frequently replenished the liter-sized common cup. The wine tasted more like port than the Welch's grape juice of my Congregational childhood. We sat, as I had years before, on the visitors' bench, but the real Baptists, eight hundred strong and of all ages, stood for the whole three-hour service.

Ilya's choir, in which Sergey's wife Olya takes part when she's not vacationing with the kids in Saratov, sang like a very good opera chorus, though they'd hardly appreciate such a worldly description. After the service we had an unfortunate meeting with a touring group of gum chewing American Baptists. They defended the war in Vietnam on the grounds that we are enjoined, in *Acts*, to support missionaries in pagan lands. My students, thank goodness, let this pass with a minimum of whispered obscenity.

In '81, at a similar meeting, the ways and means of founding a Baptist radio station in Moscow were discussed. Sergey found this kind of pushing dangerous, though he listened politely to the arguments of the more radical brothers. He told me later that a group of these activists had held a sit-in at Brezhnev's offices, demanding a radio station like that of Billy Graham, who had recently been allowed to preach in Moscow. Sergey reported that KGB agents pleaded with the Baptist activists to vacate the premises. Only then were they arrested and, ultimately, sent to the camps. The authorities, it seemed, could do without negative worldwide publicity. One cannot imagine the issue being raised in 1961.

There is a coda to this story: The office in charge of sectarian religion decided, after the sit-in, that since the Baptists only used the church sanctuary for Wednesday and Sunday services, the Seventh Day Adventists would be allowed to use the church on Saturdays. This led to internecine warfare so furious that no one had time or energy to organize another sit-in. "I wouldn't have given even *them* credit for such guile," said Sergey, laughing. Nevertheless, as a good Baptist he found the situation intolerable.

Late at night, Sergey delivered us back to the Mozhaisk campground in his little Lada, a perk of his position as editor. He wouldn't let me go without a bushel of his *dacha*-grown potatoes and a fine pair of amber cufflinks. I remain an agnostic, but promised him that only his church would be considered, including baptism, if my views ever changed.

Finally, two days late, we approached the Kremlin wall. "On Red Square every Russian realizes that Russia is his mother." According to Raya, our fine Moscow guide, Leo Tolstoy wrote that. Raya has a piquant face and a body large and out of proportion. In Russia, this tends to mean inescapably bad nutrition, not indiscipline. Raya was doing this Kremlin tour for perhaps the hundredth time, but, one felt, with undiminished enthusiasm. She was the first guide in my experience to explain the "ranks" or levels of the icon screen, the relative positions of traditional and special local saints. In the Kremlin Armory, she appreciated for us the succession of Catherine the Great's court dresses. The rising *embonpoint* brought us to see that ruler as the likely model for the ubiquitous nesting *matryoshka* dolls. How accurately Raya described the stitches, the lovely silks and velvets in the raiment of tsars, bishops, and royal princesses preserved here. It was, apparently, gradually becoming accepted to betray a loving interest in the monarchy in non-Soviet history. Tolstoy was right, Russia, not the Union, was Raya's mother.

For us foreigners, Moscow *is* Russia, as for them, New York represents the States. Red Square at the center of Russia is the lodestone that draws one here. Unseen, it was probably the concept of the Kremlin as political center that pulled. Once one is here though, it is the atmosphere created by that swirling oriental church, Vassily the Blessed, which Ivan the Terrible built to comemmorate his victory over the Tatars at Kazan. Then there are the Kremlin's steep, rosy, brick walls, towers, and the entrance gate with the clock that is Russia's Big Ben. (In 1961, our guides, Muscovites all, proudly kept their watches set at Moscow time, even in farthest central Asia, as if only Moscow time existed.)

Finally, Lenin's tomb in red and black marble, the black brick of the great square, the name of which, *krasnaya,* means "beautiful," not "red." It seems as if some word worthier than "vast" ought to have been coined for this expanse. This space electrified history once, and all those years of fearful attraction certainly color our perception of these blacks and these reds. We assumed that actions affecting our lives very decisively could be taken here, telephones raised, buttons pressed. Now, many of the departments of government have been moved to the "White House," two bends away on the Moscow river. Nevertheless, Red Square, Vassily Blazheny, and the Kremlin have not become merely museums. There is *mana* here to outlast little men.

When I first came to Red Square in 1961, my taxi driver told me of the removal of Stalin from the tomb he shared with Lenin six months before that fact became public. Interred in the Kremlin wall, disgraced by monstrous murder, his place in history, and that harsh account of what has brought us to this moment, is in no danger. It makes no difference how many of his statues are melted into pruning hooks. This may, of course, equally be said of Lenin, indeed, of Attila the Hun. No small part of the impression made by Red Square is the hefty queue of visitors lined up to see the well-pickled mummy that was Lenin.

Scoff as I will, when I finally decided to see the man, not very tall, with obviously hennaed moustache and scanty hair, I had no doubt that it was he who had channeled Russia's hunger, wounds, and war misery into John Reed's *Ten Days That Shook the World*. Of course, it may be that such *mana* depends upon a certain stock of historical knowledge. Still, in the deep impression that the dead Lenin made upon me, it was not prior knowledge, but the serious, thoughtful faces of the Russians around me, their attitude as reverent as that of Orthodox or Baptist believers, that let me feel Red Square's real electricity.

The Kremlin is, of course, the formal center of government. Nevertheless, for the historically inclined, it is one huge historical museum. For those convinced that our situation has roots, causes, and that it is "sweet and decorous," not only to die for one's country, but also to understand the reasons why, a museum may be more important than a visit to a session of the State Assembly, the Kremlin lives.

There are three main cathedrals in the Kremlin: the Archangel Cathedral, the Assumption Cathedral, and the smallest, the Annunciation Cathedral. The first contains the sarcophagi of the rulers who governed from Moscow before Peter moved the center to St. Petersburg. The remains of important Moscow prelates are housed in the Assumption Cathedral. There, the walls are ablaze with murals, some of the school of the most famous icon painter, Andrey Rublyov. It is, however, the smallest, the Annunciation, that draws me.

The floor there seems to be solid jasper, oblong russet plates, as if the floor of the universe were finite. An Orthodox church always prefigures the macrocosm, and is a universe unto itself. The *iconostas* flames with gold, the precious frames barely sufficient to set off icons limned by Rublyov and Feofan Grek, or by their acolytes. I do not use the term lightly. An icon painter, *ikonopisets*, is thought to be possessed by God. A follower, a mere copiest, is called an *ikonomaz*, an icon smearer, a mere human in his work. Grek, like Rublyov, considered an *ikonopisets*, is utterly of the spirit with his few, spare curves and dashes to suggest an astounded, saintly face. Rublyov's faces and hands are all warm ochre and yellow, with rich green, red, and blue robes on these real bodies. His saints are of this world, not ready just yet to give up the flesh, the glory of the eye, no matter how harsh the reality about them, and Rublyov painted during the worst, early years of the Tatar yoke. The lineaments of his subjects are resigned, serene, sure of ultimate justice before the Throne. They are, though, in no hurry for this last judgment. The precious stones and gold of the frames, and the rich robes hold firmly to this wracked and lovely planet, giving vibrant life to this sacred microcosm.

Ivan the Terrible, not admitted to the consoling beauty of the Annunciation Cathedral because of a fourth marriage, despite his victory over the Tatars, is said to have added the porch about the original church, decorated with a fearsome Last Judgement. From here he could watch through a small grill and listen to the service within. Indeed, this white stone universe offers comfort, very much of this world, though to the Orthodox an indication of the next.

Nevertheless, our day in the Kremlin gave us a taste for more worldly joys. Moscow provides other readings of everyday life as well. That very evening we happened upon a performance of Chekhov's *Three Sisters* at the Moscow Art Theater. The venue was the real stage, the beginning and home of Stanislavsky's troupe and method. Here, Olga Knipper, who was to be Chekhov's wife, first played the part of Masha, with Pushkin on her tongue and her heart on her sleeve, as the playwright had written it for her.

Chekhov has always been the most difficult Russian writer for me to warm up to, because he is the most thoroughly rational: Western. He refuses spiritual comfort and is utterly impatient with Russian disorder and indiscipline. Still, I teach his works often because of the economical, clear syntax, simple vocabulary like Kafka's, and straightforward thought. It was not for nothing that Chekhov was a practicing physician. These are the qualities that a novice in Russian needs. I need his rationality.

For Chekhov, we had to return from the campground, which was far from downtown. We got off the subway late. I took a vaguely remembered shortcut, using dead reckoning. We startled more than a few drunks and lovers, for Moscow is crowded in the tiny summer squares and alleys which fill the space behind the center's apartment buildings. Nevertheless, the Seagull, itself an image from another Chekhov play, came into sight on schedule. We had plenty of time to show the tickets that unusually merciful "wolves" (scalpers) had parted with that noon. The house, the old house of Stanislavsky, Nemirovich-Danchenko, Chekhov, and Gorky, was not crowded. We could even have occupied better seats had we wished.

There was only the one set, the see-through, skeletal house of the sisters, open to our gaze from all directions as the moving, circular stage displayed it. This drama, where undisciplined decency is crushed by efficient selfishness as in all of Chekhov's plays and as in Russia now, took its dreadful, everyday way before us. The gauche, utterly autistic sister-in-law ousts the cultured, dreaming sisters from their home. In doing so, she raises serious questions about mere decency, about the limits of forgiveness. Love and forbearance prove expensive, even murderous, illusions. Only Anfisa, the old peasant servant, survives in joy, because she can be content with a place to lay her head and "a crust of bread." Chekhov, physician, cool reader of symptoms, ends on that note, underlined by the wailing confusion of the finally awakened dreamers. A sparse, sufficient reality, a skeletal house: a Russian reality is the offered diagnosis.

A "downer" then, as they say, but our joys were copious, nevertheless. Half a dozen of my students had chosen Chekhov over the Bolshoi Theater's sumptuous *Swan Lake* and were not disappointed. I met an old friend, a former student now employed by United Press, with her own byline, in Moscow. This friend, Lynn, led us to a Mexican restaurant at the top of Hotel Intourist, gallons of salsa and chips, a pitcher of margaritas, and a view of half the city with my *alma mater*, Moscow State University, showing golden on the Vorobyov hills miles to the south. The whole view was handsomely tied together by the reflecting ribbon of the Moscow River. Sometimes, even in Russia, everything works.

There was a quite unexpected bonus. While Lynn gave an impromptu seminar for the students on journalism in Moscow, I got into a conversation with a pair of waiters from Zaire, budding Chekhovs, studying medicine in Moscow. My doubts about the quality of a Russian medical education were answered rationally, simply, as my doctor-dramatist might have answered. "We are African. We can afford *this* education. Zaire cannot, perhaps never will be able to equal or afford American medicine. In Russia, another third-world country, we are dealing with professors who have learned to make do. Besides, since you teach literature, you must know that Pushkin, Russia's greatest poet, was descended from an Abyssinian grandfather and proud of it!" The medical students were, no doubt, right on all counts.

On our last Moscow day, it was time to do laundry. Russia had not yet discovered the joys of the laundromat in our camping time, so after wearing the meager supply of one's unmentionables four days each - frontwards, backwards, and then inside out frontwards and backwards - it ultimately became necessary to find a water tap and washboard. Most of the camps offered these most of the time. The washing inspired helpless laughter in the Russian women similarly engaged: they had never seen a man wash clothes. One had further to keep an eagle eye upon the wash line or risk losing the here-irreplaceable unmentionables. Half a day lost, then, unless you enjoy reading nervously as the steam in the room curls your hair and pages, then jumping up to survey the wash line.

John, one of our students, found a better way. He began with a duffel that his careful mother had packed full of clean clothes and another, empty sack. Dirty garments went, slowly enough, into the empty sack. When his clean stuff was used up, he began to wear again the least dirty shirts, etc., from that same sack and so, turn and turn about, he avoided laughter-filled laundry rooms and the waste of good trip time for the whole fifteen weeks.

CHAPTER IV

Moscow to the Caucasus

There follows here a week of three-hundred-mile-a-day driving on hideous highways, navigating by inaccurate maps, over the most literary of Russian landscapes. Here Tolstoy, Turgenev, Leskov, and Sholokhov have their roots and their muse. This is the old posting road to the Caucasus, the route of bankrupt or exiled army officers. Pushkin (though a civilian), Tolstoy, and Lermontov were on their way to seek treasure and a beautiful Eurasian princess, to experience the whistling shriek of Ossetian bullets, or, as in the case of Lermontov, to find a lonely mountain grave. The Caucasus occupied the place of the American Wild West for the Russian aristocracy. For Pushkin, who was never granted a passport, it was the only experience of non-Russian culture, except for books, of course. For us, it was the first immersion in the immensity of the steppes, and in the cultural variety of the Russian empire.

On any driving day, during all of our twelve trips through Russia, there were certain chores to be accomplished. First, there was the mere driving on mediocre roads that were by no means well marked. The driver and the navigator/map-reader were seriously engaged in finding our way. Sergey's Lada was quite exceptional and, after all, belonged to his church, but there were few private cars, until the middle '80s. The government, therefore, saw no special need for gasoline stations for non-institutional vehicles, and gasoline pumps were few and far between. (Another oddity of this Soviet empire was that its gas pumps were all manufactured in Czechoslovakia.) We bought, in advance, usually in Vyborg, special coupons to entitle us to the eighty-octane gasoline that was minimal for Volkswagen vans. The khaki Russian trucks that made up most of the traffic used an extremely smoky sixty-octane fuel which would have destroyed our motors. We had to be sure, then, not to miss the rare gas stations, usually rather wretched sheds with a tiny *benzin* sign. Then, we had to beg and pray for eighty-octane fuel, sometimes kept only in twenty-liter carry-cans behind the gasoline shed. The reaction of the station attendants who would have had to walk behind the shed to get it for us was often *nyetu*, there isn't any.

A further point of no small interest: these rare gas stations were so arranged that one had to approach a kiosk, bow low because the speaking aperture in a heavy glass window was set three feet from the ground and then shout one's order sideways and upward. If and when a deal was arranged, the proper number of twenty-liter coupons had to be introduced into the speaking aperture, and the attendant reached down to examine them. If there *was* an eighty-octane pump, it would be activated from the kiosk. Finally, one gassed one's vehicle. If you guessed the number of coupons wrong, if, say, sixty liters didn't suffice to fill the tank, you bowed again. If sixty should be too much, the precious eighty-octane ran on the ground before the indifferent attendant could be brought to turn it off in the kiosk. These procedures became more complex in 1991 when, as Soviet power trembled, vendors felt the breath of the coming "free market" and demanded double payment in dollars.

Most official exchanges, indeed most official business, was carried on in a similar way. Solzhenitsin remarks in "Matryona's House" that the heavy glass window with the low aperture disappeared for a while during the Khrushchev "Thaw," but it returned under Brezhnev. Renewing, or applying for, any of the many official permissions and visas was done in this atmosphere. Even choosing groceries, then paying for them before one was allowed to touch them, worked in a similar manner, though the aperture was generally a bit higher. Further, attendants, sales clerks and lower officials tended to be almost universally morose if not violently rude. (I must, in all honesty, add that they became much friendlier when they recognized us as foreign travelers. Once, when a friend and I waited twenty minutes to be served, finally, lukewarm tea, our waitress suddenly apologized: "Oh, I'm so sorry. I thought you were Russians!" She quickly brought fresh, hot tea.)

This boorish attitude of salespeople was said to be occasioned by Marxist folklore that considered all middlemen, as opposed to productive proletarians, to be socially inferior. The middlemen, of course, struck back. In any case, the obligatory bow before the glass window made one's relationship with the vendor or clerk very clear. There is something in this forced kowtowing that, for want of a better word, I call "oriental." Whether it is bad or simply expresses the real situation between those who control goods and those who need those same goods in an economy of scarcity, I am not enough of an economist to say. For an American to bow down, though, is a very *interesting* experience. Somehow, we were always happier to buy fruit, vegetables, freshly made *piroshky:* meat or rice or plum jam filled pies that we called "greasies," at the peasant markets or from private sellers who stood with their baskets along the roads. (In our time in Russia, collective farmers were allowed a half acre to raise their own food and either consume or sell it.) Best of all, of course, was to gather fruit - apples, plums, even peaches and apricots - from the first row of orchard trees beside the road. These were, by custom, set aside for the needs of travelers. Their trunks were whitewashed to mark their use and, I guess, to make the dark roads more easily drivable at night.

After Moscow, our first goal on this southern swing was Tolstoy's estate Yasnaya Polyana. Although it took both a gentle "Good morning, ladies" at some tents, and a louder "Up, dammit!" at others, we usually managed an early departure from Moscow for the long day's drive to the Tula region. Ultimately, though, the fat little gateposts of this most visited of literary estates, came into view. I imagine that Gandhi and Schweitzer were the last world figures to be the target of pilgrimages. Voltaire, Goethe and Tolstoy were earlier victims of this immodest habit. I think it is acceptable to come here now, if not too piously.

We bought tickets and fresh raspberries measured by the glass, and waited in the parking lot for our turn to be guided through. The students, tired and grumpy at times from irregular meals and long drives, still followed the Russian explanations gamely. In 1969, we were in better physical shape than usual. For our last night in Moscow, my van organized an unusually fine dinner based upon good, dark bread and cheese (and Russian bread is simply the best) along with dried oxtail soup, *"golubtsy,"* or stuffed cabbage, and a couple of bottles of sharp Caucasian Riesling. We had coffee and Russian chocolate for dessert. (The students did much better when I didn't shop for them. In Leningrad, I bought chocolate sauce, thinking it tomato paste, for a proposed spaghetti dinner. Margaret said, "Mr. Yatzeck always buys such *neat* things.") They came to do the shopping by turns, though it was no light task, for both grocery stores and individual items, like cheese and hamburger, were hard to track down. Even bread was best bought early in the day.

In any event, we arrived at Yasnaya Polyana. The acreage that remains with the estate is part of a working collective farm. As we waited for our guide, a horse-drawn cart loaded with hay, upon which three red-faced ladies were actually singing a genuine folk song, passed by. The variety of rye in the field next to the parking lot was about my height, six feet, and ready to harvest. The overgrown yard and untrimmed trees gave the place a nicely dog-eared look, which suits Tolstoy, I think.

We were, again, lucky in our guide. She both knew and loved Tolstoy's work. That author, she let us know, lost the manor house at cards when he was a young officer in the Caucasus. A neighbor bought it, numbered the parts, and carted it away. Later, Tolstoy and his family lived in the two wings that used to embrace that building. We entered through a porch whimsically railed with white painted cutouts of hobbyhorses. The general atmosphere was informal. The first floor rooms, clean and plain, have fine portraits of ancestors, the writer and his children. I recognized only one artist. Leonid Pasternak, the poet's father, made lovely drawings of the Tolstoys, who, with the German poet, Rainer Maria Rilke, were family friends. The furnishings, as at Tchaikovsky's mansion in Klin, are fringed and Victorian. The one surprise is the shortness and plainness of Tolstoy's bed. His works made me think him as tall as Peter the Great: seven feet. In reality he was, at most, 5'4" in height. We saw his shoemaking bench, testimony to his genuine regard for skilled physical labor, and heard of his repeated 150 mile walks from Moscow in self-made boots. I was peculiarly pleased to find that the name of the estate, Yasnaya Polyana, means "the clearing in the ash, *yasen*, forest," not "clear glade," as I'd always been told. Such etymological puzzles charm me.

For me, the most impressive aspect of the estate is the writer's grave. Tolstoy explicitly asked not to have a monument, in a country much given to elaborate memorials. He wrote, however, that if there must be *something* to mark his grave, then best of all would be a simple mound at the edge of what he called "the ravine of the green stick." The reference is to a game played by Tolstoy and his brothers when they were children here. On rainy days, the boys would make themselves a house by hanging blankets and carpets from a table. Cuddling together there, his brother Nikolay dreamed up a club called "The Ant Brothers." It was, not surprisingly, a proto-communist society based upon mutual aid and love, including a special quest. The brothers swore to spend their lives searching for a magical green stick. When found, this talisman was to bring about universal happiness. It was thought to be concealed somewhere in that ravine on the edge of which Tolstoy's modest turf mound rises. The place is quiet, for the tours are so humanly arranged that only one small group of visitors arrives there at any given time. The mound, the green ash trees, and most certainly one's acquaintance with Tolstoy's thought combine to make one dwell upon just that magic wand, which, perhaps, we all at some time seek. The writer's work is just such a search.

On one of our tours, Yasnaya Polyana was closed on the day that we arrived. As Saturday and Sunday were not regular days of rest in the then-officially atheistic Soviet Union, one might at any time encounter locked doors on, say, the only day one had to visit a much desired site. The Intourist authorities insisted that we keep exactly to a planned schedule, but this schedule was often spoiled by days suddenly set aside at our tourist sites for hygiene, inventory, or repair. As a some of the students dreamed of visiting Tolstoy's estate for years, this blind lottery could be dispiriting. The Russians, who ran into such obstacles in all aspects of their lives, found our dismay on such occasions to be odd and excessive. I realize now how spoiled we must have seemed to them.

On that one time when Tolstoy's estate was closed, against both experience and reason, I approached the militiaman guarding the fat little pillars and explained our plight. Against all previous experience, he promised that the estate would be open the next day and sent us to a nearby *Soviet* campground, a parking lot on the Volkov River with no amenities whatsoever, but also with no registration requirement. As registration seemed to take up half of our Russian experience, we happily dispensed with said amenities, like plumbing. To this overnight, I owe my first conversation with a *tolkach*, just such an operator as Tolstoy despised.

A *tolkach*, a "pusher," had, in those times, the task of traveling the Soviet empire to find the steel, lumber, wire, bricks, and cement that the state industry by which he was employed needed. Usually, the need was immediate, to fulfill some aspect of the annual economic plan. He was provided with rubles, western luxuries such as *Jack Daniels* whiskey and lingerie, or, indeed, whatever it might take to induce the manager of another state industry to supply his bosses with what they needed to fulfill the plan. He was not necessarily supplied with principles.

This *tolkach*, Efrem, happened to be taking a vacation out of Moscow with his wife in a brand new Lada. The car alone, in 1977, put Efrem in the category of the well-to-do. Successful, then, quite beyond the Soviet norm, Efrem was no seeker after the green stick of the general good. Though a member of the Komsomol and soon to be a Party member, he found the proletariat slothful and uncultured. He complained that the government supply clerks' demands for immoderate bribes *ni po chinu* (of a magnitude unrelated to said clerks' importance) had become harder for him to deal with. Further, as he was paid a very decent percentage for his pains, the Soviet taxes seemed outrageous. The man could easily have set the tone for the first Soviet Rotary Club. What became clear, if Efrem were to be believed, was that the industrial production in the Union had little to do with announced goals and successes. Business here, by 1977, was a matter of well-oiled connections, absolutely dependent upon corruption. Today's *mafia* has relatively old roots.

A second conversation, this time with our guide, Ella, at the estate the next day, had an odd similarity to the campground gossip of the evening before. Ella, a graduate student in Russian literature, was to read an academic paper in Boston that coming fall and presented the estate in a much more explicitly literary manner than earlier guides, who tended to dwell upon Tolstoy's biography and family life. An emancipated Russian woman, she found the mature Tolstoy's desire to give up the estate and become, with his wife and nine children, Christian mendicants on the roads of Russia, selfish and mad. Nevertheless, she was in love with his prose, knew even the most obscure works almost by heart, and had her own view of them, as opposed to official Soviet scholarship.

After the tour of the two wings, walking Tolstoy's favorite paths, Ella dropped behind the group for a moment to ask me a question that much concerned her. She heard that the Tolstoy family in California was negotiating to buy the estate and either move everything or set up some sort of a Tolstoyan Disneyland. Brezhnev was said to be the seller. She was concerned about her position but even more alarmed about the possibility of this very Russian treasure being alienated. I did my best to assure her that the rumor had to be baseless. As I talked, though, I thought of my *tolkach* of the evening before. I realized that this neat, correct, no, *wise* person, and that rather questionable operator, had one very important conviction in common: a certainty that self-interest, not law, ruled in their country. I, for one, had not realized that the "Leninist" principles according to which the

Soviet Union was supposed to be governed had so totally disappeared. As usual, I had much to learn.

After Tolstoy's estate, it was really time for something light: an ice cream factory or a day of volleyball on some beach, even though I can't play volleyball very well. However, geography will have it that Ivan Turgenev's estate Spasskoe (Redemption) is not even a day's drive from Tolstoy's Yasnaya Polyana and far too hallowed a literary landmark to miss. Both holdings are situated on the rich loess soil, which distinguishes central Russia, a five hundred mile circle that one might imagine around Moscow. When Russians use the magic word *rodina* (Motherland), they generally mean this area, especially if they are speaking in a cultural, rather than a personal, sense. Most of the great writers of Russia's golden age, the nineteenth century, were raised on and supported by the serf-holding estates of this region. They grew up to become the repentant noblemen, haters of serfdom, who made Russian literature known in the West. Turgenev, then, was next. Volleyball would have to wait.

Once again, we happened upon the best possible guide to Spasskoe. (I began to think that provincial literary shrines offered convenient bolt-holes for thinking Russians.) Bogdanov was a man fascinated by, even besotted with, Turgenev's works. He was a fanatic, a poet, striding and eulogizing mostly outside, in the well-kept garden, pointing out spots connected with the works, knowing and quoting Turgenev's prose as if it, too, were poetry, which it often is. The students, visibly struggling to understand, were utterly won over by Bogdanov's great love for what he did. His feeling, and fantastic memory led them to do *their* best. As it happened, he spoke of the stories "Bezhin Meadow" and "Khor and Kalynich," both set within a few kilometers of the estate, and then of the novel *Fathers and Sons*, in which Turgenev's very manor plays a central role. As my students and I had, not at all providentially, just read all three works together in Russian, I could not have been happier.

We did tour the house, in the usual felt boots, but aside from the quality of the Victorian fringe-work - rather more luxurious than the homes of Tchaikovsky and Tolstoy - one room in particular troubled my mind. It was an elegant parlor with a fireplace and a handsome reading chair replete with pillows. Here, long before the birth of the writer, his grandmother is said to have struck a servant boy with a chunk of firewood when he was slow to bring tea. Then, apparently because his cries disturbed her, she smothered the felled lad with a pillow. As Bogdanov said, it was not usual in the time of serfdom to kill serfs. An occasional landowner was sent to Siberia for cruelty to his chattels. They were, after all, valuable sources of income. Here the grandmother exhibited the furious temper that seems to have run in the genes of the Lutovinovs, Turgenev's mother's family. Turgenev's mother, hardly less cruel, kept her sons in virtual economic slavery. The typical tenderness of Turgenev's works was, in a sense, a reaction against the iron fist of the Lutovinovs. (The writer's father left his wife and children early in the marriage.)

At the end of our tour, the students arranged a picnic near a lone oak, well surrounded with forget-me-nots, that the twelve-year-old Turgenev is said to have planted. While they sliced cheese and bread and sausage,

Bogdanov took me on a private walk to ask about my studies and also to tell one more story. "You know," he said, "I have attended the school of the nightingales here in June every year since the war." (Must I say that he meant WWII? In class, I must.) "It goes like this," he continued. "A mature male bird will sing the song." Bogdanov then whistled notes, which I had not the wit to catch. He continued, "A few high, hoarse squawks follow. Then the old bird repeats the song again. The following squawks may include one correct note. So on for six weeks, all evening, every evening, every summer, the young birds, note by note, by imitation, finally master the refrain, and each in his own way, in his own voice, the notes are held in common." Here Bogdanov used a phrase, which also means "as in a community."

"Why," I asked, "does an old bird take so much trouble?"

"The old bird," he answered, "does not think it trouble. Indeed, being but a bird, he probably does not *think* at all. It is rather, perhaps, that his whole being insists that there be a continuation of nightingales. Isn't that," he continued, "why we teach?" There is just now, as there was just then, no more to be said.

Later that afternoon after leaving Spasskoe, we made several unsuccessful efforts to buy a fat gray goose to roast for dinner. It turned out that every lovely goose we saw belonged to one collective farm or another. We made one attempt to find the chairman responsible for such creatures, then gave it up. Geese were, apparently, not part of the tiny free market that deals in fruit and vegetables along the road. The weather: rain, sun, clouds like mountains in a sky as low and wide as that of the Netherlands, caught our pleased attention but did nothing to guarantee dinner. In Oryol, however, we screeched to a halt just outside a grocery store, *Gastronom*, and found it, though it was late, both open for business and free of queues. The whole staff, for once not a morose *kolektiv*, helped the crazy Americans to find halvah, canned pasta with meat, sour cream, margarine, liver sausage, still warm and excellent bread, Russian cheese; indeed everything it took to make up an utterly unbalanced meal. As we loaded the back of the van, old women came up to buy from *us*. Sergey's potatoes in their large crate made us look like a peasant market on wheels.

As we consumed a heroic amount of these goodies in the camp in Oryol, we spoke, almost sang, of Spasskoe and Bogdanov, the park-like lawn with a pond and double row of linden trees there, the fine nineteenth-century ambience. Turgenev's gentle heart and vicious ancestors, how shall we resolve these?

On a later trip, we visited Spasskoe again, but found Bogdanov gone. An Intourist official in Oryol told me that Bogdanov's fiancée, who disappeared in the post-war purges, had, in the late '70s, miraculously returned from the Gulag. They were married, and Bogdanov returned to university teaching in Moscow. What a fine ending for the student of nightingales!

That time, however, Oryol had some less pleasing surprises for us. When our kids struck up a conversation with Russian students near our motel, the campground having meanwhile been closed, militiamen arrived to try to take the names of these Russians who were so intensely interested in foreigners. I said "try" because the Russians simply evaporated. Again, promised a lecture on Turgenev, we were herded into a dingy Hall of Culture and forced to listen to an interminable farrago about the new Soviet constitution. When I complained to the Intourist manager, she said that I must have misunderstood, and in any event, the lecture was good for us. As it turned out later, in Odessa, there was a use for the force-fed legal knowledge.

At 8:30, more or less, the previous night's feast on *Gastronom* bounty having slowed our morning preparations, we left Oryol for Kharkov. We were now entering the real Ukraine. It was the time of the wheat harvest in this Russian breadbasket, and impressive battalions of rather old combines, as many as ten in a row, reaped the tawny fields or were met with on the road, as they proceeded to the next collective farm. Here, too, there were the lines of whitewashed trees, apples, even the Russian favorite Antonovkas, plums for the traveler's taking, and American corn, still young for roasting, which was increasingly planted as fodder after Khrushchev's 1959 visit to Iowa. The gas stops were cleaner than in the north, and one often met farm women selling fresh *pirozhki* filled with meat or plum jam. The attendants at these stations were brasher, less morose than in the north.

In the afternoon, we passed a monument. The WWII tanks on pedestals give it away, and we decided to make a long day's drive longer by investigating. We were in the neighborhood of Kursk. It was here that the Soviet march to Berlin began in 1943, for this is the site of the Kursk "Bulge." Here, a combination of American Lend Lease trucks and a large accumulation of new artillery produced in the factories beyond the Urals made it possible for the Red Army to fill acres with cannons parked wheel to wheel and fire a frightful barrage, followed by a tank attack and send the German army reeling west.

The monument was built on top of a large underground bunker. Whoever planned it was an unusual Soviet authority, for it seemed totally lacking in that understandable but chauvinistic righteousness which marks most war monuments. Within the bunker, there is a two-meter wide stretch of sand that runs along all four walls. It is littered indiscriminately with the smashed weapons and helmets and canteens and *stuff* of both armies. The mixture of German and Russian films of the decisive battle which raged here is run constantly, suggesting quite consciously that this struggle was not just a Russian agony, but rather a general human one. It is not Germany, but war itself, that is the enemy, and that must not be forgotten. We drove on, rather quietly, through afternoon heat, harvest dust, and a mighty thunderstorm to Kharkov, where we arrived through the arc of a rainbow.

The driving days were long, ten to twelve hours, on this trek to the Caucasus. Not every day offered a Bogdanov or a Kursk Bulge. Further, the Soviet Union was experiencing a heat wave, so my tolerance for student conversation and peanut-butter socks declined rapidly. There are, usually, no nice places to picnic on this major road, much of which resembles a thousand-miles of New Jersey. On uninspired days, I had little to do but miss my summer hayfields in Wisconsin and my books. I wondered why the students didn't clamor with questions about Tolstoy, Turgenev and Sholokhov, whose home territory we were just now experiencing. I realized, at occasional moments of clarity, that I must have been irritated with them for not being *me*.

One morning, when I couldn't properly sleep, I found myself, at five a.m., combing the van for the instant coffee, which had not been returned to the crate of cooking supplies. I was absolutely shaking with rage at these thoughtless, messy, fellow travelers of mine. Anxiety built as I couldn't find my habitual drug. Why did I take these damnable trips? (Years later, I found an answer in the notebooks of Albert Camus:)

It is anxiety that is the value of travel. For at a certain moment, so far from our homeland, from our language (a French newspaper is unaffordably expensive as are also the evening hours in cafés, where we try to come shoulder to shoulder with others), a free-floating anxiety overcomes us, and we involuntarily experience the desire to return to the protection of our old habits. This is the most obvious result of travel. At such a moment we are both feverish and pervious. The slightest impact shakes us to the root of our being. Let us meet a torrent of light then and we stand before eternity. For this reason it is mistaken to say that one travels for pleasure. There is no pleasure in travel. One travels for the sake of cultivation, if by cultivation we mean the exercise of the most secret of our senses, that is, the feeling for what is eternal. Pleasure distracts us, in the same way that the "diversion" described by Pascal distances us from God. Travel, which is at once a higher and a more earnest science, leads us back to ourselves. (Camus, Albert. *Tagebücher: 1935-1951*. Rowohlt/Hamburg 1972. p.14. My translation.)

***

When I travel with my students, the rut I fear to lose is the culture of books, but our Slavic tour does rub my nose in, makes me *pervious* to, the realities of culture, nature, and human intimacy, to the reality which Camus calls the *eternity* of these things. I will try to explain how I was made ready to understand Camus.

At college, culture is a classroom exercise for many of the students. On a camping trip in Volkswagen vans, the students want to relax, to be democratic, to avoid cultivation and culture as much as possible, because these things are felt by them to be duties. It may be that they cannot admit, in their peer group, in public, any supreme interest in cultural or educational values, which are, after all, *not* democratic. As a group, they talk about food, drinking bouts, fraternity functions, and *fun,* or they plug into Walkmans and listen to hard rock. This maddens me. These are not *my* people.

However, on this day when I couldn't find the coffee in the early morning in a Ukrainian campground, I found the following *books:*

Turow. *Presumed Innocent.*

McDonald. *The Gulf Stream.*

I also found more serious things:

Stone. *Prose Style: A Handbook for Writers*

Konwickij. *A Dreambook for Our Time.*

Tolkien. *The Lord of the Rings.*

Rybakov. *Children of the Arbat.*

Shaw. *Man and Superman.*

Arnold. *The World at War.*

Rilke. *Letters to a Young Poet.*

Tolstoy. *Anna Karenina.*

Chatwin. *The Song Lines.*

Andric. *The Bridge on the Drina.*

That was the book menu in the middle of one trip in a muddy Ukrainian campground. Even before I found the coffee, I felt not quite so righteous. The reality, the eternity of the students, was not so very different from my own.

About this same time, somewhere in the steppes, I got a further lesson in solidarity and humanity. One of the six boys in the van my colleague, George, named "The Young Bulls" for its occupants' audacity would always freeze at the passage of a jet fighter - fairly frequent here on the Russian prairie - freeze and become pensive. One evening I asked him why. He admitted to a passion for the air that was utterly at odds with his father's insistence that he continue the family's long and honorable tradition in the law.

"Mr. Yatzeck, what should I do?"

I am, by family tradition, utterly unmilitary. My great-grandfather dodged the Franco-Prussian War, though a sharpshooter in the Prussian army, by rubbing sand in his eyes and thus procuring a medical discharge. My father, having seen a GI flip a grenade into a pen of Japanese prisoners on Okinawa, implored, no, ordered me never, never to enlist, as he had. War, I guess, is the mark of our very own human, not bestial nature, since extremely few animals engage in true war, the organized slaughter of their own species. Still, I told my student, for I think this true, "You must choose the life, the profession, that you most love." I think he did. I advise all of my students this way, and my own four children, too.

This same van, "The Bulls," took me in when my own bus voted me out for back seat driving and general interference. (Our democracy went that far.) I was not very happy about this. Jim, trip bookkeeper and bus leader for the "Bulls," then taught me a lesson on the limits of professorial authority. Hurt by my unceremonious dismissal, I asked him how he managed his own unruly van. (Their mascot, a dead scorpion found on the rocks where we once made camp, swung on a thread from the rearview mirror above Jim's cherished figure of the Buddha on the dashboard.) Jim said, "Look. I can call them assholes when they act like assholes. You can't."

The Kharkov campground, after the rain and the rainbow, was a sea of mud. We dug dinner out of the back of the van, which meant Skippy and black bread, by then an uninteresting combination. With my tent under my arm, I was met first by a group of my students who asked if it would rain. *Must* they put up tents? I said it wouldn't rain, my elbows told me this. Then I was stopped by a group of Russians who offered apples and "informal conversation." As it turned out, they had rented a small cabin for the conversation, brought vodka with the apples, *and* worn suits. I rather thought that they were provocateurs. (Repeated experiences of the Kharkov campground led us to believe that either the KGB had a training camp in Kharkov, or there existed in the town a particularly zealous group of Komsomol agitators.) These "students" began with me by relaying an utterly horrid report of American racism from a very reliable American tourist whom they met. What was *my* opinion on the daily lynchings in Vermont? I could hardly deny racism in the States, though 1969 Vermont seemed an unlikely site for lynching, but did know how African students were treated in the Soviet Union, and particularly in Moscow. Nevertheless, avoiding the pitfalls of "you're another," I simply said that any American who washes his country's dirty linen in public in the Soviet Union is behaving like a traitor. What, for instance, was I to make of the Moscow student who told me that even after Khruschev's attack on Stalin's crimes during the Twentieth Party Congress an immense system of prison camps still existed in Siberia? Why, I wouldn't believe him, for no real Russian would say such things to an American guest, *even if it were true.* These "students," visibly embarrassed, departed shortly thereafter, in the driving rain, which I had *not* predicted. I finished their vodka, ate an apple, and brought my sleeping bag to the nice, dry cabin. I had briefly considered sharing the mud in which my group was resting, but decided that even democracy did not require this of me.

The next morning at 6:30, the night rain had stopped. I found the kitchen and brewed tea. It was Indian and good. Then, I had a long talk with an elderly physicist from Moscow who loved the mysteries of Georges Simenon. He was just then reading John Updike's *Centaur,* and found the book, and American writers generally, even O. Henry (a school text in Russia), too existentially gloomy. This occurred in *Dostoevsky* country. He went on to explain that Russian novels depicted decent people in bad situations, but hardly viewed humanity as negatively as the Americans seemed to do. He was able to borrow new English and American novels from a special library for physicists and had a lovely English accent, the result of working with British naval officers during WWII.

I talked literature, he physics. He said I looked too young to be thirty-six, then supposed that the ease of American life must be the partial cause. I found him a very sprightly sixty-seven. We agreed that camping and vodka keep one young. As he was tenting, I did not admit to the previous night's dry cabin. Later, when I greeted the rising students, they seemed to know that I hadn't put up a tent during the downpour and were a tad standoffish.

Our day tour of Kharkov provided contemporary interest. The municipal theater is built in the shape of a caterpillar tractor to celebrate this city's industrial specialty. Of more interest, however, was a demonstration of African students carrying posters decrying the rickety dormitories in which one of their number recently died in a fire. Our Moscow Intourist guides were horrified at the *bad taste* shown by the Africans in bringing such complaints *publicly*. This was, indeed, the one true protest march that I ever saw in the Soviet Union. There, in Soviet times, whatever was not allowed was forbidden.

On this Kharkov tour, I realized the killing sameness of most war memorials, eternal flames, uniformed children changing the guard like clockwork puppets, and then the kilometers of factories and blocks of cast cement apartments, although I ought to have known that *any* apartment was a vast improvement over half a room in a pre-revolutionary hovel. The new buildings did suggest progress, no matter how slow and unbeautiful. Further, the war and the government's attempts to repair its damages were real. I remember a tiny circle of turf in a small town in the north. We stopped to buy the bread and cheese for dinner. I strolled over to examine what looked like a small public garden, hedged in by stones. It was, instead, a graveyard. Each of the eleven stones was engraved with a different first name, then the surname "Ivanov," and the date was 1943. Entire families died in that war. Still, the present poverty of the system was almost unimaginable, in its general ugliness, though south Chicago is no Eden. The war was, then, twenty-five years back in time, so long before that Russians, privately, doubted its efficacy as an excuse for present conditions, which were improving much too slowly.

What are Russians privately? "There is," Yury Zhivago is told in Pasternak's novel, "a Marxist style. You harm yourself by openly flouting it." I am reminded of my wife's opinion that I would do better at our small college if I would use "we" in speaking of the institution instead of the "they" with which I tend to refer to all authority. There is no doubt that I harm myself with that style. *That* harm is, of course, not at all comparable to Russian dangers.

Our next campground was a park in the midst of Rostov-on-the-Don. The Don is Sholoxov's river, shallow, fast, and cold. We swam after a long game of volleyball in which a Russian pick-up team easily trounced us. Having lost fifteen pounds, I volleyed and spiked quite passably. I knew my weight because a major amenity of every downtown street is a public scale. For ten kopecks you can check yourself any time. However, all of the scales did seem to read differently. I suppose that their presence testified to some long-forgotten state health plan.

The Rostov camp, though central, was set in wet, marshy woods. This was, nevertheless, pleasant because it was easy to set up one's tent a bit out of sight of the others and avoid the military camp effect. We ate borscht and more borscht, and for dessert, the first small, perfectly globular, excruciatingly sweet watermelons. There was a sort of gazebo in this small woods, almost a full moon, talk until three in the morning, and no feeling of weariness. The famous Russian questions were "What is to be done?" and "Who is to blame?" I had an especially open conversation with Vadim, a local tourist guide.

We spoke of our wives, of the point of raising children in our time, and the things we loved to do. Vadim complained of American tourists who found fault with everything Russian. "I can agree about Soviet architecture, but they don't even like *borscht!*" He told of his middle-class antecedents and the need to deny them if he hoped to "get ahead," about his desire for an acre, a house, and time to paint, to be a professional artist. He said nothing about "the new Soviet man" which was much on his tongue when he was on duty. I knew from Vadim himself that he would be called in by the KGB to report our conversations. I heard that previous guides classed my colleague George as a violent anti-communist, me as a fellow traveler. Vadim, in private, simply laid aside the Marxist style which, among peers, he was expected to maintain. I have met many Vadims, some in America.

Could it be that our students, privately, are also sensible, worried, wondering, and interested? That is, of course, a rhetorical question. I have spoken, one on one, with many such students. Perhaps they harm themselves by abandoning the student style in public. I wonder about the difference between police and peer groups. Perhaps I am angry at Aristotle's definition of man as a political animal. Of course, students, Russians and I are *both* political and private.

That July in Rostov we were invited to a meeting with Soviet youth. Our Vadim and I attended with maybe ten students. Such meetings were seldom enlightening so George and I didn't make them compulsory. We found about ten Russian students in the House of Culture, in the "Red Corner," with the usual three-foot plaster bust of Lenin and three older leaders: two thirtyish Komsomol members and a man of maybe fifty who was a Party member. We leaders, *starosty,* or elders, sat in a row against the wall, the students sat in mixed Russian-American circles before us. They conversed, in a stilted way, about language study, politics, school, and the possibility of war, the necessity of peace. The older Party member, who clearly made the other Russians nervous, seemed to find the student talk innocuous enough, and so decided to go after me. It turned out to be my fault that the warmonger Reagan was president. The fellow *was* a bit drunk.

I got political. I suggested that a Russian who would publicly degrade Brezhnev, to foreigners, was little better than a traitor. Similarly, I claimed, an American who allowed his president's name to be impugned was also a traitor. This worked, here as in Kharkov. It always worked. The guide Vadim and the two *komsomoltsy* agreed smilingly. The Party type apologized! I had been, here, just as political, just as phony as the Russians. I really thought that Reagan *was* a warmonger. With me, too, at least in Russia, and sometimes at home, honesty sometimes remained a private matter.

Whatever the case, *private* meetings with Russians were the prime prestige items on all of our Slavic trips. As they gradually tired, students missed tours, even meals, but most of them learned, as their Russian improved or they found occasional English speaking natives including black marketeers, to seize every opportunity for private conversation. Some of them even disappeared for an occasional night in a Russian home. George and I, too, tended to rate the trips in terms of such encounters. None of us, finally, trusted or much valued public, official interaction.

The last run, to the mountains, cut across the rolling, treeless Don steppe. Here, too, angled squads of combines scored the wheat fields, but herds of horses and some horsemen also appeared. Could they be Cossacks? Inspired, perhaps, by this thought, we had a food fight with a truckload of Soviet soldiers. We had been following a khaki truck, and most trucks were khaki there, for half an hour. The back of the vehicle was full of Russian soldiers. A snub-nosed white-blond trooper, the Ukrainian stereotype, finally whipped a potato at our windshield. Before I could think, my troops had slid back the van's sunroof and flung several rather old apples in among the Soviet khaki. I said, "Pass 'im," to avoid further exchanges. Nevertheless, my tail gunner managed to land an overripe plum right in the middle of the windshield, where, recognizable by his hat, an officer was riding. We rather squealed wheels then, but there was no further fire.

Late in the day, we stopped to pick apricots as, earlier, apples and plums, from the whitewashed travelers' trees. We sat beside the almost still stream of a nameless rivulet to picnic on watermelon, white *brynza* (goat cheese), apricots, and water from a cold well. The well had a real crane, a long pole with a weight at one end. One pulled on the bucket suspended by rope from the high end of this crane, let the bucket fill down in the well, then pulled the bucket up with the help of the weight at the other end of the crane. Is that why the water tasted especially good? Or was it because, on the southeastern horizon, the crests of Pyatigorsk's five mountains had begun to show?

Pyatigorsk *means* "Five Mountains," outliers of the great Caucasian range to our south. The novel *A Hero of Our Time* is partly set there, and a mortal duel in that book seems to prefigure the author Lermontov's death in a similar duel on Mashuk, the mountain just above our campground. The camp lay in a green wood. The trees and the stars beyond them seemed an unearned luxury, as did their indifference to us, their quiet refusal to be mere background to my mood. A group of Russian alpinists were singing down slope, fifty yards from my tent. Their voice and guitar work made the Red Army Chorus seem bumbling and sloppy, but they had the advantage of the trees and the stars.

After a city tour, we bussed from Pyatigorsk to Kislovodsk to taste the carbonic waters, a nineteenth-century nostrum still favored by Soviet aristocrats: *nomenklatura*. One filled a small, flat pitcher at a wide circle of brass faucets in a lovely, tiled pavilion, then drank from the spout. Next came a half-hour stroll to assure the healing effects of the water. Kislovodsk, like Pyatigorsk itself, is a much frequented vacation venue, bountifully beautified with flowerbeds, blossoming trees, and ponds. Most Russian roads, indeed most of the cities, are dusty wastelands, but flowers are greatly loved here, and the parks and monuments are richly decorated with blossoming shrubs, annuals and perennials. They are also well kept, and there is not much litter.

This is an exception to the general rule that public conveniences: toilets and bus stop shelters, say, tended to be trashed. Other exceptions were all locations mentioned in Lermontov's *A Hero of Our Time*.

Most striking was the fact that almost any Russian with whom we spoke knew the novel in intimate detail, was proud to live in Lermontov's landscape, and spoke of that author as if he were a saint. This is true of the neighborhoods of Tolstoy and Turgenev as well. A deep respect for writers and literature contrasts with the widespread American view of literature as entertainment. In Russia, *belles lettres* alone tended, in the nineteenth century, to be believed. The strict censorship made honest political and historical writing almost impossible. Only literature, which commands nuances difficult to censor, was, and still is, seen as a source of honest opinion.

Similarly, writers and intellectuals generally considered themselves to be primarily engaged in resolving, or at least wrestling with, Russia's problems. Self-expression was often a secondary consideration. The Russian word "intelligentsia" referred more to the civil endeavors of artists and teachers than to their assumed intelligence. It is, perhaps, for the reason that Tolstoy, Turgenev, Lermontov, and many others were engaged in an effort to civilize Russia that they are still respected, still seen as a lay priesthood.

Our second day in Pyatigorsk was spent at a collective farm: apples, pears, horses and tractors, Holsteins, milkmaids, and a number of old American-made combines. The Russians expressed heartfelt, old-fashioned gratitude for these machines. They were built in Illinois before WWII, and, of course, our group didn't make them. At the same time, it was foolishly warming to come across even machines that were like those in the Wisconsin village, Genesee, where I first saw them when they were the cutting edge of grain harvesting.

A local journalist guided us to the farm, took notes, and, no doubt, wrote a feature story. As we drove our vans across a pasture, since there was no other direct road, a detachment of Red Army men on maneuvers pointed their rifles, pretending to aim at our vehicles. At once, the journalist, a man of about fifty, was out of the van, across the intervening brush and cowpats, and upon them. How *dare* they even think of frightening sacred guests of the Motherland? This journalist must also have exhibited some sort of Party authority, for the troops marched off at the double, and the journalist returned to the van filled with victorious righteousness. Because of this quality, unfortunately, he immediately turned on me as *starosta*, or elder.

What did I think of that swine Pasternak? Had I ever read such awful drivel as the writings of Solzhenitsyn, of whom all Pyatigorsk, the place of the writer's birth, was ashamed? I admitted to a taste for *Dr. Zhivago* and *One Day in the Life of Ivan Denisovich*. "How can you read such obscene shit?" my journalist inquired. Though not looking for trouble, I could only answer "Why obscene? Have you read these works?" His reply: "Certainly not! Both authors are traitors to our Cause!" quickly embarrassed him. He had destroyed his own argument.

The collective farm, for once not a showpiece, was a messy, normal, working farm. Old milking machines, Armenian combine operators who would go on to the next farm's fields when they finished here. Their salty humor and ferocious appetites reminded me of the "hired men" of the farms of my youth. Janet, one of the students who looked out for the group when I was being blindly professorial, begged us all an evening meal which was gladly granted and then wanted to stay forever: chicken, gravy, cabbage soup (*shchi*), fresh, dark bread, compote and home-canned pickles. This was a feast, and somehow a victory over the blind stupidity of the journalist, who seemed as pleased to share the farm's bounty as we were. Maybe, we arrived at "Peace and Friendship" beyond the cliché. Everyone seemed to have relatives in the States, to remember eating Lend Lease beef during the war, to feel grateful toward these odd Americans who were actually trying to speak Russian. I've seen such country hospitality only in the Wisconsin villages of my childhood.

I was up at six in the morning the day we left Pyatigorsk. (Early rising is a cheap way to gain righteousness.) Packed and waiting for my troops to arise, I got into conversation with five Ossetian bus drivers who were roasting *shashlik* around a breakfast fire, beef, tomatoes, onions on spits, drinking tea, and waiting here to replace their colleagues when the latter should arrive on route from Ordzhonikidze: the true Caucasus.

My knowledge of Ossetians consisted of the fact that Stalin was half-Osset, half-Georgian, but I wasn't about to raise the spectre of his crimes. Rather surprisingly, the drivers began a conversation by asking if I were a "Christian." In Russia, this generally means, "Are you Orthodox?" I pleaded agnosticism, and all five were noticeably *hurt*. When I asked why, one of them said that since I spoke Russian, seemed friendly and even civilized, they hoped to find in me a fellow believer. Nevertheless, the drivers proceeded to share their beef and tomatoes, ran off to find several cold bottles of champagne, and so entertained me that I was brought to admit the existence and power of, at least, St. George, patron of men, travelers, farmers, and, of course, Ossetians. I further promised to remember them whenever my ears should ring, for that would be a sign that they were drinking my health "somewhere in our magnificent mountains!" This love of the land, not the same as the system, was endemic throughout the former Soviet empire.

Steve, my right hand, drove the first half-day on the final run to Ordzhonikidze, now renamed again, Vladikavkaz. Many Russian places, given the names of communist heroes after the revolution, reverted to their former titles since the collapse of Communism. I navigated on the basis of what seemed particularly meander-prone maps. The true Caucasus begins with Vladikavkaz. The drive was hot, dusty, and slow. We fell out of the vans like peas too long confined in the pod, pulled sleeping bags off the van roofs and crashed. When the night air and stars woke us, our leader George decided to slake his thirst with cold champagne, though the camp store was closed and the gates locked up. He had, being hasty when flouted, two of his boys lift the gates from their simple hinges, then drove right out over them to find the necessary fluid. I, still watching the stars and the night, was sought out by the camp manager and warned that he was about to call the militia to punish this act of "hooliganism." (The Russian cognate sounds much like our word.) I thought quickly, for me:

"You must do your duty," I said, "but I want to tell you about our *starosta* first. He was born an albino. If you look closely, you will see that he has the typically reddish eyes. Of course, he has suffered the well-known racist slurs of his fellow Americans all his life. Only here, in your great democratic system, can he feel free."

My quick and tasteless lie was accepted so avidly that I knew I was dealing with a true believer. This assuaged whatever conscience I may have. The manager not only omitted to call the police, but helped George and the boys to restore the gates when they returned, *with* the bubbly.

CHAPTER V
Georgia and Black Sea

"The Georgian race, which represents the oldest elements of civilization in the Caucasus, is distinguished by some excellent mental qualities, and is especially noted for personal courage and passionate love of music."

"Georgia," *The Encyclopedia Britannica.* 11th Edition.

Driving in Russian Georgia imparts all kinds of lessons. The country is, first of all, in no sense Russian, or even Slavic, but a completely different mountain culture, Orthodox since the fourth century and with a language neither Indo-European nor Semitic. Georgian is said to have seven words in common with Basque. As in the remainder of the old Union, everyone had been forced to study Russian in school, but our students found it pleasant to speak with Georgians because for them, too, Russian was a foreign tongue, and difficult.

Our traveling from Ordzhonikidze was both serpentine and uphill for half a day, until we reached the Pass of the Cross. Here Margaret and I watched a large, brown eagle float up to us, from the south, and then slant off, at fifty yards, into the mists. It is not often that one overlooks an eagle. We stopped to clamber down beside the road to a famous medicinal spring,

Narzan, said to be Khrushchev's favorite, in order to "drink at the breasts of the Caucasus." The sulfurous draught somehow matched the largely mineral, even cubist, surroundings.

We stopped, too, because the mere half-day on the Georgian Military Highway had worn us badly. Much of the road was under repair, great flat plates of stone with serious gaps in between reduced us to placing first one front wheel of the van, then the other, beyond the gaps, in order to avoid a mortal somersault. Nothing edged the three thousand foot drop-offs, but occasional pitiful fences of sticks and twine. We drove through small mountain torrents, which cut directly across the roadbed. In the higher reaches, we regularly chose between dark, damp concrete tunnels built to protect spring travelers against avalanches and ruinous open roads that, though narrow, offered better visibility. Even an earlier break, sitting in the warm sun, on the snow, under Kazbek, the second highest of the Caucasian chain, had not much restored the energies taken by the fearful driving. (It should be noted that Kazbek, at 16,545 feet, is only two thousand feet lower than Elbruz, the monarch mountain, and that this latter is higher than any of the Alps.) Certainly the mountainous nature of this landscape separates it from Russian culture as well. Mountaineers tend to be their own, cantankerous kind of people.

It was said that in Stalin's time only his own people, the Georgians, did not pay income tax. (In fact, no one does now who can possibly avoid it.) Stopping at a wine cellar, a dim, cobwebby, genuine stone cave, to buy white wine for the evening meal, we met the bearded winegrower, proud of his rows of oaken casks, but seemingly even prouder of the many newspaper and glossy magazine portraits of Stalin, whom he much resembled. He saw the Great Leader's murderous ways as one of the necessities of government, nothing more. "Anyway, Russians need a stern master," he said. This was in 1969, but in 1997 many a Russian with whom I spoke said the same. It should be noted that this Georgian was speaking of *Russians*, not Georgians.

Just beyond Pasanauri on the Georgian Military Highway, we camped in a wide, dry arroyo with a narrow streamlet under a cement bridge. This situation shouted "flash flood." We ignored that shout. The rocks of the Caucasus resisted our tent pegs. We weighted down the tent edges with the rocks. We were young and inventive. The Intourist guides, far from Moscow, abetted us in this "wild" camping outside any official campground. Even now, the ugly bridge, the arroyo with its narrow, silt-milky stream, the black rocks and the red dirt of Georgia are quite clear in my mind. These details hang there like the cozy little house in the glass globe after the snowstorm subsides.

All day my student, my friend Walt, had been trying to buy a lamb for shishkebab. Stopping his VW van wherever he saw red tile roofs or even a single hut beyond a black rise, he would run cross-country to bargain with *kolchoz* chairmen or shaggy herdsmen. No luck! My green van followed his gray one hopefully, we were sick of thumbed Skippy even on crusty Georgian flatbread. We wanted meat.

After noon, after roadside apples, aforementioned bread, and Skippy washed down with homemade Caucasian cider, Walt abandoned his mutton search to lead a pilgrimage straight up a small mountain, along a foaming rivulet. The pilgrims then sat happily under the lip of a miniature Niagara and sang:

I don't want a pickle,

Just want to ride on a motorsickle,

And I don't want to die,

Just want to ride on my motorcycle.

***

It was the 60's. We sat under the splash and spray, boots and all, and sang along. Then, we shook ourselves like rained-on collies, climbed dripping back into the vans, and renewed the southward search for lamb.

In 1969, the Caucasian roads, and especially the Military Highway, were guarded. The Ossetians, who have, since the breakup of the Union, heavily promoted a political presence in those mountains, were already seeking recognition through sniping and bridge blowing. These actions took place among black cliffs upon which, as often as not, "Long Life to the Great Stalin" was blazoned in whitewash by Georgian patriots, though "The Mighty Leader" was sixteen years dead. Georgia, like Russia, offered a warming lack of rationality, taught life as embodied ambiguity. This, just then, suited me right down to the ground.

Mary Linda, *my* van's Walt, decided to photograph the next bridge we came to. It was sufficiently dilapidated and covered with skinny cows. Privately owned beasts, they were not allowed in the *kolkhoz* pastures.. Since the photographing of bridges was strictly forbidden, we might be Ossetian agents or even the CIA planning a raid, Linda, certainly against my advice and without my consent, opted for a sneak snap out the van's window. The van halted and she clicked her Leica, a hairy militiaman appeared from behind a black boulder, opened the van's front door and snatched her. Waving a rusty rifle, he retired, rather like Scylla, behind his rock.

I took this in from the van's rear seat, slid quickly enough into still-sodden boots, belted out the side door and followed the steaming trail around the black rock. There, in a rough stone guardhouse, were three empty champagne bottles, the Leica, Mary Linda, and the hairy militia sort. The guard's interest seemed to waver between Mary Linda and the Leica, so I quickly agreed to give up the film and left abruptly with the fuming girl and the camera. We jumped in and zoomed out across that rickety bridge, black cows lunging in all directions. As I hoped, the militiaman was too drunk or bemused to shoot.

That day's stretch, from Ordzhonikidze to Pasanauri, was not lengthy, maybe two hundred miles. The mountain gradients, though, and the road surface across which we had to pick our way like barefoot children in sharp oat stubble, slowed us. Walt's pursuit of the perfect roast delayed us, too. It was early evening when we careened into Pasanauri.

As fate would have it, a scraggy, Gypsy-looking man stood on the one paved street and sold lamb, practically ready for the spit. Though offended by the ease of purchase and prepared state of the meat, as his idol was self-sufficiency, Walt halted and bought. A further roadside purchase of onions, tomatoes, and eggplant finished the prospective feast. Then, we drove right on past the *specified* campground and straight out of town to find the ominous arroyo.

While, as I've said, some of us tautened tents with rocks, the here-useless tent pegs came into service as skewers. The vegetables and the mystic lamb, broiled over odorous cedar, went down well with the Stalinist's Abkhasian white wine. The mountain stars seemed both gem-bright and regally detached. The sky between was as black as stone.

Tbilisi (Tiflis) was our destination. Here, for a change, was a stone motel, showers, and a small restaurant, all crowded between the Caucasus and the road. Walt's bus hit out for a disco after dinner, while I dallied with George, our primary fearless leader. We were tired enough to sit over the remains of our *yulyakebab* (lamb burger) while drinking strong Georgian tea "to the seventh sweat," as Russians put it.

A *dzhaz* combo that followed the lamb burger attempted a big band sound. As they were only three: saxophone, bass and drums, their attempt was predicated on an ability to turn up the volume of an ancient PA system. Their "A Train" simply didn't leave the station. It began to look like an early bedtime. Next to us though, at a separate table, sat five bronzed, heavily moustached and eyebrowed Georgians. To our unaccustomed eyes, they seemed almost identical except for a finely graduated silvery-gray about the temples. They were square set, dark suited, and tieless, wearing striped shirts. We watched them arrive in a heavily finned Buick convertible of the middle '50s. In the Soviet Union of 1969, there was no legal way to obtain or own such a vehicle. We saw a dozen, more or less, like it in *Soviet* Georgia, which followed its own rules.

These men were drinking *Tsinandali*. I know this because I recognized the label and because it was the only wine the house afforded. That's why George and I were drinking tea. The Georgian roads and rocks had worn us more than we knew, beyond mere sleep, and if we didn't share any confidences, we split a common torpor. (Although I taught with him for thirty years, George was then, as he remains, inscrutable to me. His bright, flat, gray eyes, high cheekbones, and expert knowledge of linguistics still strike awe and terror in me. "Everybody is abused as a child. I enjoyed it." That is a Smalleyism that leaves my liberal poses in the dust.) Nevertheless, the five men, *mafiosi* in today's Russian parlance, replaced our lethargy with a lively common interest, and we easily agreed to try the *Tsinandali* ourselves.

We drank the wine from generic Soviet snifters. These Georgians drank Russian style, "in a salvo"(*zalpom*) a water glass at a time. When the *dzaz* group made smithereens of *Bei ,mir bist Du sheyn,* baldly stolen from Benny Goodman, the moustached ones struck: they began to sing. It appeared to us, though we lacked any experience of Georgian music, that they sang in five parts. Perhaps the notation and minor sonorities of the once famous Spanish monks give some idea of their tone, but the songs were sad and fierce and sweet by turns or all at once and were not reminiscent of monasteries. In short order, the five men literally drowned out the PA system Johnnies, who slunk away.

Then George and I, the only other guests in the restaurant, were treated to such a concert as only the well-loved earth, not heaven, can provide. We knew no Georgian but these five men, close-fitted and tuned strings of one instrument, evoked what seemed to me exactly that pity and fear that the chorus in Greek drama is said to have effected. Whether they sang of love or death, one could, in their honest presence, imagine no other singing, no other life. Conviction, not entertainment, was the burden of their praise.

Still, the singing gradually altered, for the group continued to down white wine by the glassful, while George and I, no haters of alcohol, left our glasses sheerly untasted. The music, then, gradually changed, and in the following way, in the course of what seemed an hour, a moment, or a day, the chorus gradually became a quartet, a trio, duet, solo and silence. One after another, from youth to age, the order seemed to run and the singers slid, more or less gracefully, to the splintered Soviet parquet. When the patriarch finished his solo and lay slumbering, an athletic look-alike waiter set to work. He gently rolled, slid, and coaxed each of the singers, in reverse order now from age to youth, out of the hall and to an appropriate bed. In the almost-humming silence of the afterconcert, in that *tristesse animal*, he gathered up *twenty-five* bottles into a wheelbarrow with the dinnerware, and finally, the tablecloth as a covering, left the hall. Then we felt that we could leave, too.

At dawn, as we left the motel *Tbilisi* to undertake a city tour, a gathering of moustached men in striped pajamas serenaded the balconies of the wing where the American girls stayed. In five parts, fiercely, in shapely stanzas, they evoked real love, real death.

***

Because colleague George's bus, the cursed Gray Goose, had lost its third windshield, our last spare, we all went first to the very modern, then, "Iveria" hotel to rent a Russian sedan for the Goose's occupants. "Iveria" is the old Roman name for Georgia, but although the hotel was much nicer than anything in Moscow in 1969, the attitudes there were pre-Roman. Rental rates were twice Moscow's, and when our Russian guides demurred, the Georgian manager said "This is Tbilisi, not Moscow, and you needn't rent if you would prefer to walk." That settled matters.

Tbilisi itself has gray, stone-block churches with faceted central domes. There are, of course, icons within, but their beauty lies mostly in the engraved and enameled icon frames. This silver work, along with a particularly brilliant style of enameled miniature, was much closer to what we were to see later in the museums of Istanbul than to the north Russian religious art. As in the political portraits of our time, the saints in Georgian churches tended to have Georgian features, just as pictures of Marx or Nixon, in China, look Chinese.

After the formal tour of Tbilisi, some students and I went walking. On a small hill, though most of Tbilisi's are large, we came upon a Georgian bakery, a stone silo sunk fifteen feet into the ground, a charcoal fire at its bottom, and two bakers kneading dough into flat, round cakes and slapping them down against the hot sides of this odd oven. I still don't know what made the bread stick to the stone once it was baked, but the bakers unworriedly raked the flat loaves up, gave us a crusty one to nibble, and warned us to let it cool first. One of the girls admiringly ran her hand along the well-set basalt wall of the bakers' storehouse, experiencing the texture of the stone. I resolved to give her an "A" for such loving learning. Stone is well worth knowing, for it makes up the mountains.

After "doing" Tbilisi, we arranged for two excursions: to Gori, Stalin's birthplace, and to Mtsketa, the older Georgian capital. In Gori a tiny two-roomed log hut, under a steel roof to protect it from the weather, was the shoemaker's "cabin" where Stalin, Joseph Dzhugashvili, was born. The hut was appropriately proletarian, and it was no surprise to learn that Stalin's education was a religious one. Indeed, the priesthood offered the only inexpensive route to advanced education in pre-revolutionary Russia. It is also no surprise that the ranks of the revolutionaries throughout the nineteenth century were filled from the families of priests and from the religious seminaries. These "*popovichi*" may have learned the thirst for justice from the Bible, but what is most striking about them is their quite exceptional refusal to expect, as the Orthodox generally do, that justice can be left for the Last Judgment. These priests' sons were quite "Western" in their expectation that a change of power could resolve Russia's millennial ills. We see now that neither Soviet nor free market ideology has succeeded.

Across a dusty square from Stalin's family cabin is a large, wedding-cake style museum. This architectural horror was filled to bursting with portraits, prints, banners, carpets and inlaid wooden tables and plaques. Enormous statues of the Leader stood everywhere, surrounded by jeweled, gold, silver and crystal tributes from the world's potentates. It was a four-story trophy cabinet, so to speak, and here, as in Russia, the pride of the museum guides lay in the evidence that someone important in the West had actually recognized Stalin's, and Russia's, existence. The significance of this inferiority complex can hardly be overstated and must not be ignored if one wishes to understand Russia.

After Gori, the Intourist guides suggested a stop at the ancient capital of Georgia, Mtsketa. This old city, blessedly devoid of Soviet architecture, is warm yellow stone, unapologetic and seemingly aware of its ancient, genuine nobility. Here was the ruin of a monastery on a high hill overlooking the town from the west. The hand-chipped outline of the church and the honey-colored limestone of the walls were enlivened by the quick lizards affronting slow time. Then, there is the fortress-castle with its bulls' heads from the period when Romans bivouacked here, Mithra worshippers all. The cathedral within contains the *sveti-tskhoveli*, the life-giving pillar after which the church is named. One feels neatly poised on the cusp of paganism. Best of all, though, was an afterthought of one of the guides, Mamulashvili's garden. This was simply the gift of Lucia who, having seen it before, felt that we should not miss it.

Mamulashvili means "son of the Motherland." Now deceased, he was in 1969 a ninety-six-year-old landscape gardener of international repute, off in Europe designing yet another park when we came to Mtsketa. It was his pleasure that his personal garden be opened to the public on certain days of the week, when this was convenient for him and for his German lady acolyte. This was, as far as I know, the only privately owned extensive pleasure garden in the Soviet Union. I think it no accident that it is in never quite subjugated Georgia.

There were tiger lilies, roses, cacti, rocks of strange and lovely hues and shapes, narrow paths, violets - every sort of flower. It was like a Japanese garden for elegance and style, but more overgrown. The skull of a mountain sheep with the great two-and-one-half turns of gray horn overgrown with philodendron is somehow particularly impressive. What an unwarranted pleasure it seemed, there in the Union, to wander quietly in this quarter acre of private, hospitable space. For those few minutes in Mamulashvili's garden, one felt housed, enclosed, exempt from the exigencies of travel. I rather imagine that this is a major function of gardens. I even suspect that etymology would support this.

Mamulashvili's living monument was free in all senses, except for the need to keep it beautiful. It had nothing to do with "them," the State, unless "they" chose to come, as we came, as Mamulashvili's guests. Georgia seemed generally to be wondrously beyond Russian schizophrenia. One spoke with a Georgian and, public or private, he was all *there*. Perhaps the distance from Moscow, the freedom of the Black Sea, and the mountains themselves played parts in this unquestioned assumption of personal liberty.

This freedom also took less aesthetic forms. Georgia produced wine, cognac, tea, tobacco, and fruit: luxury items, and much in demand. A kind of *mafia*, even in 1961, sold these luxuries across Russia. It was said that the Metropolitan, head of the Russian Orthodox Church, bought truckloads of wine for his Moscow cellars. Georgian *biznismeny* were able to arrange for the use of state-owned vehicles, or even whole trains, when they needed transport. Further, in 1969 we saw 1950 Buicks and Mercury convertibles on the mountain roads, but never in Russia proper. Once, a carload of Georgian sports pulled up beside our traveling van, on a rather narrow stretch of mountain road, to hold up a case of cognac. By gesture, they offered to trade for our pretty, hennaed guide. Steve, my sensible driver, demurred. Their gesture was crude, even beastly, but argued a kind of rough independence not usual in the Russia of 1969. Now, these 1969 sports seem but the fathers of today's "new Russians," the *krutiye* : "the abrupt ones."

On our return from Mtsketa, we gave a hitchhiker a lift. His name was Nimrod, and he was a very proud Assyrian. He found us an obscure gas station when we needed hard-to-find fuel, then led us behind to picnic tables beside a small, tree-shaded brook. There, we ate spicy Georgian soup, lamb *shashlik*, fruit, and baklava. We paid a modest two dollars apiece, although Nimrod was crushed when we would not allow him to treat us as his guests.

Georgians, the many other ethnic groups of the Caucasus seem to be at home in this land though Stalin's purges killed Russians and Caucasians indiscriminately. Only provincial Russians seem even nearly so rooted. In Moscow, no one is at home. There, "they," the ones who fly the flags, seem omnipresent.

After Tbilisi, our route led to Adler, on the Black Sea. The road is at least smooth macadam. Great iron gates open into tea and apricot plantations. Water buffalo, as in Bulgaria or Rumania, work muck farms to raise maize and what looks like sorghum. Tractors divided the work with gaunt "personal" horses, and "private" cows lay everywhere on the road shoulders where the grass was free, not collective. Soon the palm trees of a rather northerly tropic area appeared. The Black Sea is all Russia's Cancun.

We camped and roasted our flesh on black beaches consisting of three-inch white-striated stones. We carried on lazy conversations with Russian factory workers whose state-controlled "unions" ran vacation camps here all year round for their members. Transportation and vacations were provided free of charge. The students stretched out, genuinely relaxed on the beaches, and even colleague George seemed to love these intervals, but I found them rather boring. Then again, I'm a hidebound northerner. More to the point, I look terrible in a swimsuit. For this time, serious conversation died. Florida is, after all, a time for mindless "spring break." *I'm* a bore at a beach party.

Adler did possess one unusual sign of western modernity. Long after Khrushchev's visit to the United States, we found here one of the supermarkets that he tried to make a state imperative. An airplane hanger an acre square held perhaps twenty fifty-yard rows of shelving. Half of the shelves were filled with greenish jars of apricot marmalade, half with yellowish boxes of macaroni. Ten immaculate white-capped, utterly bored sales ladies stood behind ten modern cash registers, which replaced the omnipresent abacus. Out in front of the *Supermarkt,* a lone, raggedy entrepreneur caught all of the possible customers with his ice-cream cart full of small, frozen Algerian chickens. Like the Christmas oranges that were available in Moscow in 1961, these chickens had, the man said, been bought with Soviet tanks, a kind of universal currency - and a fateful one. Russians on vacation eat chicken, not macaroni, judging by the length of the poultry queue.

Though we kept no particular schedule in the beach camp at Adler, the Russians, or at least some of the Russians, did. At seven a.m. a loudspeaker trumpeted, and after the Soviet National Anthem, a very martial lady gave exercise commands. Russian women in black, one-piece bathing suits dutifully stretched, bent, and bicycled in the air. Their other halves were noticeably absent. This seemed, to me, the same resolute, hopeless battle that Russia herself - and was the land not she? - had been fighting for a millennium. Again, it was the women who fought.

In the evening, when the black stones of the beach became chilly, there was a beach café. One morning, when the café finally closed, an East German paraplegic in a wheelchair returned with his wife from an evening perhaps too relaxed. We began to talk, and he poured out, very loudly, though in German, a denunciation of the Soviets (one thousand years behind) of Russian exploitation of the D.D.R. ("Our wives must work to support *their* 250,000 occupation troops"), and of the Allied weakness that handed their half of Germany over to the Soviet Union in 1945. It was a tirade, not a conversation. His quiet wife tried to hush him, as, too late, did I, but there was a German-speaking Russian woman who, it turned out, denounced him. I found out later that he was expelled from the Soviet Union for "wanton defamation of the socialist bloc, before Western witnesses." He would probably lose his well-paying position as a draughtsman in Dresden.

A witness to these matters, a teacher from Berlin and a Party member, explained the seriousness of the charge when we met again later in Lwow. There, we left camp separately and spent the evening walking and talking in the formerly Polish, now Russian, countryside. We talked about teaching and books, about students and their failings and our failings as teachers. He spoke of the Pope, whom he and his family had fortuitously met in Krakow, before Karel became Paul. Then he described the way in which some teachers got their students to incriminate their parents by asking, not if they tuned in to West German television, but simply what the shape of the clock on the wall in the news broadcast was. The western clock was square, as I remember, the East German clock, round. This was the Dr. Bauer who hoped that I knew which side I was on. I told him, as I said to begin with, that the "free" world was better.

Dr. Bauer's complaints of socialism were, except for the clock story, not largely political or economic, but cultural. He felt that Russia was both too foreign and too primitive to manage central Europe effectively. This is pretty much the case that my friend Dieter in Hamburg makes against the United States as leader of the Western alliance. I find, now, that I am on the side of this ethical, warm, and literate German, but that I cannot entrust my thought to any ideology. As well founded as Dr. Bauer's attacks on Russia as ruler of the East may have been, he knew little or nothing about the failings of the "free market" West.

It fits here to write also of a West European fellow traveler, *sputnik*, met in the camps, who also had something to teach. A large, outgoing Hollander, underway with his wife and small daughter (who called her father and me "the two bears" for our size and "growly" voices), clarified a repeated joy of the Russian trip, the many-domed churches. He was an agnostic too, but he said, "Only when we again build great cathedrals will we return to civilization." I found, I still find, his words utterly true.

We camped three days at Adler, another two at Sukhumi. The Sukhumi camp was not on the beach, but beneath a suspension bridge on a lovely, fast, pale-green river. Here swimming, not roasting, was the accepted activity. Sukhumi does offer a monkey farm where experimental animals are raised for the use of a research institute, and we always visited this institution. The local guide was proud of the medical breakthroughs attained here. Mostly though, doubtful that much progress could come of such a bad smell, we swam, partied, and rested. The local Ossetian boys were less reserved in their approaches to our *geerls* than Russians in the north. They seemed to have inherited grab-and-run tactics from earlier nomadic invaders. I spent, sometimes, more energy than I could afford defending the ladies. They, in turn, didn't always appreciate my efforts. One co-ed told our bookkeeper Jim and me, "I like to be touched! Is that a problem?" It was, probably, a new and necessary lesson for us to realize that nowadays one has to be *asked* to be a White Knight.

Suxumi camp staff tended to be Caucasian mountain types. They also tended to be, for want of a more exact term, romantics. The curly-haired and much moustached young camp manager came to me in the early evening to ask for an introduction to one of the coeds. I said that I was not a pimp. Embarrassed and explaining that the desired favor was a common one in Ossetia, he asked me to come to a friend's house to make peace over a glass of Sukhumi's famous, and rare, "black" wine. We set out in his Lada in quite a sporting mood, but the friend, alas, was not at home. The moustached one then made the wine quest an affair of honor, always strenuous, usually hopeless.

Three other friends confessed to empty cellars. This wine is, it seems, never found in retail trade, and we even searched my host's own house. His wife and eight-year-old black-haired daughter, both stunningly beautiful in the slim and doe-eyed Caucasian manner, made me puzzle at his ardent wish to meet my coed. Still, it was, no doubt, the foolish, omnipresent taste for the exotic, the other side of the fence, which drove him. He was, of course, not alone in his senselessness.

At perhaps two in the morning, we found, at still another friend's mother's house, two bottles of the required beverage, not "black," when held up against the moon, but rather a dark, arterial red. We drove then to the riverbank. "What about asking your Ann to drink with both of us?" he asked, hopelessly. I thought it too late to invade her tent, and said so. There we sat until dawn discussing women and their vagaries. At such times, the evil fate of men seems, really, to be the necessary result of their own driving stupidity. The stories of women that we exchanged did nothing to contradict this axiom. Never can we accept, I guess, Occam's razor. Never can we choose the simple and comfortable. Always must we have the rarest black wine, whatever the intensity of the following hangover.

Our last camp before boarding a Black Sea motor-ship with our vans was Sochi. In the generally prudish Union, we got an odd shock when we gave two young women a lift and soon realized that they were what we now describe as "partners." They were vacationing. Now in Russia, or Georgia, homosexuality is rather more brutally despised than it is in Bear Creek,

Wisconsin. Nevertheless, this pair was quite out of the closet.

The real charger of the two, the woman who came right out on the road from a crowded bus stop to snag a ride with us, was an architect, a specialist in city planning. In Russia, this generally meant the symmetrical placement of poured cement apartment blocks in a rigidly mathematical order. Our architect, however, gave us a love song to Riga and Tallin, demonstrating with unfeigned rapture how two Latvian ladies in wide skirts maneuver past each other in a narrow medieval street, expressing her utter adoration for such outmoded, vital building. Her friend, a quiet pharmacist, spoke about the dreadful difficulty of obtaining antibiotics from the West without hard currency and of the suffering that this lack entailed.

Most unusual was the breadth of their world-view. Taking us for lunch to a genuinely traditional Russian restaurant, they spoke, not of gay rights, but about the contrast of the Tudor-style timber and rubble architecture of Riga with the Byzantine roots of Russian church building. I, not at all missing the usual ideology, warmed to their vision of the varied beauties they'd had the luck to see. We learned over a fine Russian lunch how their well-earned broadness of view implicitly criticized our sometime failure to appreciate the freedom of thought and behavior that was supposed to be our birthright.

In Sochi, our Intourist guides demonstrated another aspect of free thought. Our vans were already buried deep in the hold of the motor-ship *Ukraina*. George and I were, quite unreasonably, asked to furnish the license numbers of our vehicles if we hoped to purchase passage for our students. Otherwise, there was a possibility that our vans would travel ahead without us. Two professors, we hadn't the foggiest notion of the numbers. Our Intourist ladies, Ella and Lucia, quickly wrote out a list of the seven plate numbers, as George and I gaped. "You don't even drive," we said. "How did you think to memorize the numbers?" Ella, having led us out of hearing of the ticket clerk, said "Numbers, schmumbers. We made them up. They'll never check, the vans are in the hold. It's too much trouble." We learned how freedom is there to be seized, no matter how apparently encumbered.

Waiting for the *Ukraina's* departure on the beach at Sochi, I was shaken by the integrity of a portly Ukrainian woman. Burned brown, barely covered by a tiny orange swimming suit, she looked like a wrinkled toad. In a moment that singing poet's voice prevailed upon one like the sudden beauty of Gawain's Loathly Lady. She described -- no, painted for us the Ukrainian end of the Carpathian Mountains, her home ground. Suddenly, one understood the magic of that fine film, *Wild Horses of Fire,* which was made there. She explained the jealousy with which an old Russian woman had taken Jim's table umbrella, he was hated for being able to afford the bottle of German beer he was drinking. On Ukrainian independence, since achieved, she said, "Unless we can arrange for gasoline from Azerbaijan there'll be no independence. We can't live without our Ladas!" And grinned. About Lwow, and the Poles who want it back: "It was ours long ago!" Of the younger generation and private land ownership: "They don't want the collective farms' land. They want Western goodies without work." Her father, a professor at the Pedagogical Institute, knew eight languages. She knew "only" four. Her recent effort had been to raise a stone memorializing her father's achievements. Only a few of his former students had, so far, been willing to help. Still, they would raise that stone! The lazy young were, after all, not evil, but somehow lacked "true desire." (And I?) She, Lesya Romanova, seemed to be one of Auden's "just." The architect and the pharmacist, our Intourist guides, Lesya Romanova: are *all* Russian women as admirable, as free under pressure, as these? (It's true that freedom tends to raise its head far from Moscow.)

Finally, we were en route, Sochi-Yalta-Odessa, on the *Ukraina*. First off, there was the relief of not driving the horrendous roads. Then, there was the neat, orderly life, announced meals, lack of road shoulder grit in the food. Are ships everywhere as orderly as here, surprisingly, in Russia?

We cruised for two days, two nights. The second night was the "Talent Show." Annie, a great favorite of mine, entered. Mascaraed to the hilt, cigarette in mouth corner, she scorched out a torch song: "Ain't Misbehavin'." She was followed by a Hungarian couple in tuxedo, and a long, lacey gown, who didn't demonstrate but lived a *csardas* and, in so doing, proved again that true art takes everything, is not done "off the cuff."

Politics "off the cuff," in Yalta at least, doesn't work either, when it runs into Lesya's "true desire." I acted as translator for a Russian guide, Yakov Abramovich, when his regular translator called in sick. When he showed us the hospital named after Jean Paul Marat, I interpolated a *precis* of Marat's death in the bloody bathtub to the utter joy of an English-speaking group of Czechs who clearly lacked revolutionary piety. Lenin's redwood, a gift from the United States, became a proper place for him to have been hanged. More joy. I thought myself quite the fellow.

After the waterfront tour, Yakov Abramovich offered to do a literary turn with me. He brought me to the place where Tolstoy, Chekhov, and Gorky famously held discussions on the beach. We toured together the house-museum of Chekhov. We discussed the writing of Isaac Babel', whose *Red Cavalry* is my favorite modern Russian work. Yakov Abramovich spoke of his years as a set designer in the Soviet film industry and how, in the "Doctor's Plot" period before Stalin died, he'd lost that work because he was Jewish. Then, perhaps *a propos* of films, he suddenly burst out: "How *could* you elect a B actor, like Reagan, president?"

Now, I was no Reaganite, but as I've said before, the etiquette of such a situation then, in the Union, was to defend one's country, one's turf. I asked Yakov, in my turn, why he had elected Stalin?

"I lost my family, and my work, under Stalin," he said. "The ones who did not die in the purges were killed in the war with the Fascists. At the end, like Babel, I cultivated the conversation of silence. You *know* that no one *elected* Stalin, but *you* are supposed to be free. You are our hope for peace. How, again, I ask you, could you be so *frivolous* as to elect that second-rate cowboy actor president?" And he wept.

Then, I didn't think myself such a fine fellow. I felt as though it were I who lacked "true desire," honest zeal for the good. I had been the B actor during Yakov's tour. In Russia, politics may be anything you like, but when they are a joke, they can belong only to the category of *Galgenhumor*: the sneer of the executioner or, more often, the rictus of his victim.

CHAPTER VI

Odessa, Kiev, and Over the Border

When Ben, one of my students, was flushed sweating from his tent by a summer freshet in Luna, the Netherlands, we should have foreseen a hot, wet summer. When the buzzing and chorusing of flies and earwigs damped down the dialectics of a lecture on the new Soviet Constitution in Oryol, we should have predicted a buggy one. Taken together, damp heat and insects ought to have warned us to double our supply of Lomotil, our anti-diarrhetic of choice. Slavic in title and nature, our student campground did nothing to forestall disaster. It followed, then, that a day after arriving in Odessa, we sat on a sandy beach by the Black Sea and waited for the hospital to release eight of our companions who were learning patience and serenity through a mass visitation of amoebic dysentery. There were also rumors of cholera.

Russian medicine is not the point of this story. Its burden is, rather, the depredations of the Soviet brand of police state. Friends idle enough to be curious about our adventures camping with our students in the Soviet Union always begin with "Weren't you scared?" Joe McCarthy and Ronald Reagan, not to speak of Arthur Koestler's *Darkness at Noon*, have conjured up an image of the Russia of that time where even the dogs and cats, when not a part of the menu, were police informants. This, then, is a story about being arrested, an extremely infrequent occurrence during our twelve campaigns through the Soviet Union. I'll try to make the most of it, just to meet conservative expectations.

It began, this near-Gulag experience, with dysentery on the Black Sea beaches. Students were dropping like flies. Intourist, our Russian host institution, sent three white-coated "medics" to tell us that we were ill, because we hadn't been taught to wash our hands before dinner. They brought us a table and four chairs and set them neatly beside the water so that our group of thirty-seven could dine above ground level. They lectured us on cleanliness and godliness, standing beside steaming heaps of human excrement droning with flies, but the camp's physical conditions did not present possible sources of infection to these thick stethoscope wearers. After their presentation, the three walked off west along the beach. A government trio of manatees would have been as useful.

Predictably, the students continued to drop writhing to "damp Mother Earth," travel by "Quick Help" van (*skoraya pomosch*) to the nearest hospital, and recover after a three-day regime of semolina grits and salt water. They did find the hospital beds considerably more comfortable than sleeping bags but would have preferred to enjoy the city. Their care, being Socialist, was free of charge.

Diana, my wife, then still my student, looking ahead, as is her unfortunate wont, said: "No matter how sick I get, I don't want to go to a Soviet hospital! Never! Just make me bouillon with – ech! - raw egg..." Two hours later, having lost breakfast out the front flap of her tent, she wheezed, "Okay. Call *Quick*

Help."

I called. The small *Quick Help* van appeared in a leisurely fashion. I begged to accompany Diana, colleague George would mind the store, and we were whisked together to District Hospital #17, a close neighbor on the bay of Odessa. A grizzled, silent, one-eared gnome drove. The wounds of WWII are everywhere in Russia. A Clark Gable look-alike male nurse tucked Diana up on the wheeled stretcher, took her temperature, and cooled her forehead with a damp towel. I squatted on my heels, a common and useful art in Russia's south, and tried not to roll out the open rear port of the ambulance. Clark looked closely at Diana as he laved her greenish skin, and then at me: "You're too old to be her husband. You her teacher?"

"I'm her fiancé."

"Too old! You old capitalists take all the pretty girls."

"Picasso married a woman forty years younger than he was. And *he's* a Socialist."

"Who's Picasso?"

"Okay. Charlie Chaplin, then. Movie star. A British Communist. Married a woman thirty years his junior."

"Chaplin is a comrade, but what are you?"

"I'm an anarchist, if you must know."

"Stalin would have had you shot; you're too old, I say."

We finally came to the hospital. Clark bummed a whole pack of Marlboros. Then, smoking, he rolled the now somnolent Diana to the receiving area. A young doctor with black, curly hair, his rank evident from the "Head Doctor" embroidered on his long white coat, took charge.

"Is this the foreign girl?" he asked. Head doctors don't come to meet just anyone, even under Socialism.

"Yes. My fiancé. Amoebic dysentery is my guess. Nine of our students have come down with it."

The doctor, having made his own quick assessment, agreed. "I've seen some of your students, but this is more serious. Her fever is high. She may have a serious case." This was no joke!

I was allowed to remain in the hospital with Diana as her translator. Her Russian, even then, was more than fair, but she was in no condition to talk. She was given a medication, an antibiotic, I imagine, and hooked up to a saline IV. The young doctor had her placed on a high, leather table-bed equipped with a strategically placed aperture. Her case was, it developed, indeed more serious than those of the other students. That first hospital night the IV could just keep pace with her loss of body fluids through diarrhea. A nurse came and made up a pallet for me beside her bed. The curly-haired doctor appeared at half-hour intervals and administered, near dawn, another injection.

"American. Hard to get. Damned good. Only for tourists," he said of it. By nine a.m., after ten hours on the table-bed, the crisis seemed to have passed. I got up the nerve to ask, then, about the danger. The young doctor shrugged, waved a deprecating hand. "With cases as serious as this, the chances are 50/50. *She'll* recover. Good American antibiotics."

We spent five days recovering at District Hospital #17. I met the mother of a child with an eye infection, and then the husband of a terminal cancer patient. Hospital rules, it appeared, allowed relatives to tend their own sick if they wished. "Speeds recovery," said the monosyllabic young doctor, "and we're always short-handed." I thought this feature of Soviet medicine a clear advance over our less relaxed procedures. However, it developed that there was some hesitation about allowing me, a foreigner, to remain with Diana in the hospital. Our nurse, Darya Ivanovna, soon a good friend, solved this one. She whipped out a white coat like the young fellow's, also embroidered "Head Doctor," and threw it at me. "Now, if anyone asks, just say 'nichevo' (it doesn't matter), and wave your hand the way *he* does. Then go to the gas shelter for a smoke. That's what all the head doctors do."

I did. It worked. My cover was never blown.

Diana's total recovery was predicated upon the drinking of several gallons of salt water every day and the consumption of buckets of semolina grits (*mannaya kasha.)* The IV stand with what Diana claimed to be bent, rusty needles came into operation whenever her consumption of salt water flagged. I, on the other hand, was served the best Black Sea perch or stuffed cabbage and potatoes, and a variety of fine Russian soups well garnished with sour cream. The quality of soup, in Russia, is directly proportionate to the amount of sour cream floating on its surface. As we ate together, my diet did not improve Diana's mood, but she bore this with seeming patience. She *did* grimace, though, when Darya reported that the cook was pleased to have a healthy *man* to feed.

The five days passed pleasantly enough in conversation with Diana and Darya. Diana mostly talked about salt water or gurgled faintly. Darya, a young-looking grandmother in a country where, as I've already said, forty-year-olds often look sixty, raged at her daughter's children for their "moped madness," their insane lust for motorized bicycles. She wished, she said, that *they* could have experienced, with her, the nine hundred days of the siege of Leningrad by the "Fascists," the frozen potatoes that made up much of the menu. Then, she blanched and whispered, "I, sinful one. An evil wish! Some of the children were eaten then." Soon, however, her serenity returned. The pride of survival, the splendor, in memory, of a ferociously hard time endured, had toughened Darya and her many sister *babushky*. Any minor disaster - an insulting doctor, ne'er-do-well son-in-law or drunken husband - could be borne with that dismissive wave of the hand so typical of Russians. Of her husband, she said, grimly, "Love's no joke: you can fall for a goat," a phrase that sounds better in the rhymed original. To Diana she would say, "Drink your salt water, Dianushka. It's only for a week. Soon, you'll be walking the golden streets of your America." Her voice betrayed no envy at all.

When visitors or authorities neared Diana's room, Darya would send me to the doorway of the World War II gas shelter, still so designated, for a smoke. From the butt-strewn porch, I could overlook most of Odessa, once a thriving, multilingual port. I thought of Isaac Babel's *Odessa Tales* where Benya Krik, Jewish gangster extraordinary, celebrates his sister's wedding with smuggled Spanish sherry, French *paté*, and Havana cigars. The author describes *himself* as a green youth with "*glasses* on his nose and Autumn in his *heart*." In response to Stalin's Soviet hype, Socialist Realism, Babel invented what he called "the genre of silence." After three years of practicing this economical genre, the author was shot. For boldness, he need not have envied Benya Krik.

After five days and the return of Diana's vital forces, we felt ready to depart, to catch up with George and the group in Kiev. Our ward doctor, though, not the young man but a hulking "Big Nurse" sort (Darya thought her cut out of roofing tin and about as deep) insisted that we complete a two-week quarantine. This was really impossible. Our VW van of students had waited for us and missed most of Kiev. More importantly, our Soviet visas would run out before the two weeks were up, and we had barely time now to reach the Polish border. Masha, one of our Intourist guides, stayed with the students at the campground. She thought it would take many days to arrange another exit visa. We had to get to Kiev, and out, at once. On the sixth day at Hospital #17, having been refused by the looming "Big Nurse," Diana and I hunted out the hospital director's office to appeal to Dr. Roman Nikitich Serdyuk, the Director. That is, we went over Big Nurse's head.

"Two weeks *is* the usual quarantine period for dysentery. However, we know the impatience of tourists, and " - here Dr. Serdyuk simpered a bit - "of young ladies. I grant your release. *Bon Voyage!*"

We returned, probably too triumphantly, to Big Nurse. She turned a dark brick red, said, "Nonsense! That Roman Nikitich...!" and added, "I categorically forbid you to leave!" Nevertheless, when our students made their daily visit, we sent them right back to camp to pack and alert Masha the guide. We asked them to pick us up at noon, when Big Nurse generally took her break.

It didn't take long to pack our hospital belongings. Then, I made a quick run to the *kolkhoz* market down the street to buy farewell flowers for Darya. When the students returned, we took our leave. "*Proshchaite,*" we said, that final good-bye in Russian which means, "forgive us any evil done." Darya just grinned and said, "*Do svidaniya*": "until we meet again." Darya knew Big Nurse.

We almost made it to Kiev. We drove about 450 of the 500 kilometers. At this point, we were flagged down at one of the frequent GAI posts: Government Automobile Inspection. We found ourselves arrested for "illegal departure from Odessa District Hospital #17." Then, two-car relays of police, one ahead of us, one tailgating, escorted our van back across the nine GAI districts which separate Kiev from Odessa. Now, it rained, the heat finally broken. Funny, but scared, the students joked about runaway feces. Masha, the guide, looked as green as Diana had a week earlier. I wondered if Big Nurse had a brother who ran the Odessa jail. Diana, though, rather resembled a newly slimmed, salt-water-dieted, redheaded powder keg. She was, I think, too angry to feel fear.

It was midnight when we were escorted through the hospital gates, swung especially wide for us and our escorts. A night crew of nurses and supervisors, all women, all strange to us, sat in judgment, cast-iron replicas of Big Nurse. We met Darya in the entry. She'd finished her double shift and was heading home for tea and sleep. She said, simply, "Allo! I said so" and waved her roses at us, smiling.

The lynch mob of Big Nurselings decided that since we had all taken part in the violation of Diana's quarantine, we were all to be considered exposed to amoebic dysentery. We would, as a group, have to undergo rectal examinations, scraping for samples, and await the morning laboratory results. As laboratory reports for Diana had taken at least two days, we understood this examination for what it was, a painful vengeance.

This medical coven further declared that since we must be presumed infectious, we could not return to the campground. As the hospital had no vacant beds (in my occasional wanderings I had come upon three vacant *wards*), we would be forced to sleep sitting up in our van, guarded by GAI men. When Masha, an unusually brave Intourist guide, explained our hasty departure by the imminence of the lapse of our exit visas, one of the witches hissed, "*You* are a Soviet citizen. Be silent!"

Diana utterly refused to be scraped again. I, out of solidarity, followed her example. The other students, free in all but life and death matters on this most independent of tours, agreed to the ritual scraping in hopes of catching at least a flying glimpse of Kiev on their way to the border. Diana and I would, presumably, be making a prolonged stay in Odessa.

At this juncture, desperate or inspired, I remembered that forced surprise lecture on the new Soviet constitution in Oryol. Arrested, I had the right to call a lawyer. Big Nurse's surrogates simply denied the fact of our arrest; we had only been "taken into custody and made subject to prophylactic sequestration." Diana, fighting fit by now, snarled, "Call the embassy in Moscow!" I demanded this international right of all foreign travelers. The white crows looked thoughtful, but only for a moment. Quickly, one of them "remembered" that the telephone line to Moscow was under repair. "Then we'll report this illegal imprisonment at the embassy in Warsaw," said my formidable young fiancée. I translated. Wonderfully, the examinations, rather thorough to judge by the red eyes of the already examined students, ceased. For a while we sat, seriously exhausted from much driving and much scraping, in a large closet furnished with straight chairs which was just adjacent to the examination room. We didn't look forward to vertical rest in the van.

Suddenly, (*vdrug*, mainstay of Russian suspense writing) Diana's monosyllabic young doctor *happened* by with a bottle of Armenian cognac, a bowl of fresh cucumbers, and permission to party and/or crash in an oddly overlooked vacant ward. I didn't even try to discuss the effects of cognac on dysentery patients with him, let alone that of fresh cucumbers. I agreed, in the course of the dancing and song that ensued (the young doctor happened also to have an accordionist with him) to meet formally with Director Roman Nikitich Serdyuk, with members of the hospital's Board of Trustees, and with Dr. Olga Ilitchna Kapralovna, alias Big Nurse, the following morning at nine. (Following? It was already four a.m.) Roman Nikitich hoped, our young doctor was now quite loquacious, at least, dared to hope, that we would, with the traditional generosity of Americans, comrades-in-arms of the Great Fatherland War, accept Dr. Kapralovna's and his own deepest apologies and regrets for the violence mistakenly done us. The hospital would be more than happy to make up, in any possible way, for...

"Gas coupons," said redoubtable Diana, in Russian.

"Gas coupons," said the young doctor, in English. He had, until that moment, betrayed not the least knowledge of English. "Gas coupons, impossible to find anywhere, shall be yours," and he kissed her hand. I couldn't *wait* for him to remark on my age.

Danced out, slept out, we met the patient hospital trustees at eleven a.m., two hours late, after a "normal institutional breakfast" of smoked sturgeon, buttered French bread, caviar, red *and* black, apricots, and that marvelous globular watermelon. We accepted apologies, especially Big Nurse's roofing tin words, for the "unaccountable error." We accepted enough gas coupons to get us not only to Kiev, but well beyond the Polish border. We probably swore eternal brother-and-sisterhood. Then, at noon, we finally mounted our van. Darya, who had come to see us off, said, "Now *proshchaitye*, farewell, don't remember our evil doing." As should be evident, I have and I have not.

***

This *caesura* stands for what we missed in Odessa during our hospital stay. It would be a great, even mortal, error to deny my colleague George and his beloved opera space just *here*, because of the special provenance of the opera house in Odessa. This lovely port is memorable for much more than its hospital.

There was, in the nineteenth century, a Vienna firm that manufactured and delivered prefabricated stone opera houses. In our wanderings, we have enjoyed Donizetti, Verdi, and Leoncavallo in such precincts in Sarajevo, Lwow, and Odessa. These small gems show our George, *Opernmeister par excellence*, to best advantage. Any town, *stanitsa* or *Dorf*, possessing even

151

one drunken tenor was a possible venue for opera. George wangled tickets. Decked out like an Esterhazy for the Russian opera, he was a sartorial delight. He managed unwrinkled full dress out of a single flight bag, which also harbored ten cartons of Camel straights. Whether *Pagliacci* and *Cavalleria Rusticana*, the usual central European summer fare, or Rimsky Korsakov's *May Night* (a real bummer), the crystal chandeliers, gilded baroque boxes, and champagne glasses reflected, though they could hardly magnify, our *samoderzhets*. George's radiant pleasure utterly convinced the lowest boor among us of the value of high culture. Who could disdain such limitless joy? It must be added that the adoration of the opera, the concert stage, the ballet and drama form no small part of life as we observed it in Russia. Older ladies, in modest, but stylish black, appeared out of the most unimaginable rat holes for every serious cultural event. They testified that the arts, along with the church, had triumphantly survived tyranny in Russia. For the *intelligentsia*, a very Russian word, the arts have always meant truth rather than propaganda, or even experiment. They still do. George led us to all that truth.

***

Our second try for Kiev featured driving rain, abrupt green hills, then flat, rich fields of the Ukraine. Earlier, near Oryol, we had seen fields of poppies and sunflowers. Here, a month later, we saw wheat, cherries, apples, currants, and blueberries, all this fruit for sale, even in the downpour, along the road. My colleague George ordered and paid for an Intourist motel supper of *solyanka,* a cold soup with dill, olives, beef, chicken Kiev (really), tomato salad, white wine, ice cream and especially tasty coffee. He himself was off, with his bus, on an expedition to Sholokhov country.

Well fed, we set up our tents next to those of the group in a *bor* or grove of tall, red pines. We already managed to admire Kiev's chestnut trees on the high bank of the Dnieper and been politely informed that tourist dollar stores here were called "Chestnut," not "Birch," as this was the Ukraine, not, and don't forget it, Russia. At 7:30 p.m. I was wiped out, struggling to get my tent up when Lucy came to tell me that George's bus had died again, 117 kilometers out of Russia's first capital. We bussed to another camp where Ella, George's Intourist guide, and Charlie, our Bible merchant had hitched to seek aid. Although we'd sworn not to drive at night because of drunks and the mannerly habit of turning off headlights when Ukrainians meet another car at night, we set forth. Ella lit Camels for me, worried intensely about George and company, and recited Lermontov, which is a good deal more ominous than Pushkin.

When we arrived at milepost 117, George had already been hauled away by the mechanic's van. We finally caught up with our colleagues at the Kiev city limits, and delivered a pack of Camel straights amid grateful tears. George had been sniffing snuffed matches in lieu of cigarettes, and he proudly led the procession back toward our camp. On the main street, *Kreshchatik*, the route along which Prince Vladimir drove his people to baptism in the Dnieper, my clutch cable snapped with a sound like that of teeth falling out of a very old and tired mouth. It was 3:30 a.m. I waited there on an empty corner for Lyle, the mechanic, to come and get me, much entertained, congratulated, even toasted by street cleaners. As good fortune would have it, the United

States had just then made the first successful moon landing. The Russians happily let me listen to radio reports of the successful U.S. arrival on the newly conquered satellite. When I was finally rescued by the mechanic's bus, George had rented a motel room for me, the unsuccessful but well-intentioned deliverer. I should add that those Russian street cleaners showed absolutely no jealousy. One even said that he found it supremely rational to supply one's people with refrigerators and *then* with sputniks, as we had.

There was a great feeling of relaxation and pride in the Ukraine, softer people, and a softer language. By this time, and maybe this is the major drawback to camping in Russia, our energy and interests were largely taken up by the search for a good market, hot water, and the possibility of dry underwear. I was always pleasantly surprised at the communal helpfulness of most of the students, at their willingness to aid each other with tents, minor wounds, etc., at the sharing of scarce commodities and, most of all, time. They seemed to me more generous than I remember being at their age. Living with them, I felt cared for, helped, even, sometimes, kept from obvious stupidities, by equals.

For example, one of the group, himself a jazz fancier, had heard of a good church choir and made sure I knew about it. I thought I'd try to find the Saturday evening service though I hadn't a clue to the church's address. (As I was mapless in Kiev, an address wouldn't have helped a lot.) I soon found, however, that the omnipresent sorority of widowed *babushky* who rule everywhere in the East were also connoisseurs of choir music. They simply passed me from hand to hand, when I asked for the best choir in Kiev, and I quickly found myself at the Cathedral of St. Vladimir. This church was even older than the Kiev Sophia, but it was redecorated in the Russian variant of *art nouveau* at the end of the nineteenth century. The choir, high in a balcony and across from me, looked rough and dowdy, which is comparatively high praise, and, of course, they sang like Slavic angels. What basses! I could sing along only because I had a cold. I was also tired, sick to my stomach, runny-nosed and extremely dirty, as was, just then, often the case with us campers in the Ukraine, I have never enjoyed a performance more. The cathedral was very crowded, and there were many couples, thirty or younger, for whom a number of baptisms were performed. This occurred in 1969. Kievans seemed to do as they liked.

On the way back to camp, I met a plasterer for whom I was "his third American." His first had been a Negro from Wisconsin, a leading artist in the Kiev circus, and his "second," was a G.I. he met at the Elbe where they shared a weekend victory spree. I, his "third," would insult him deeply if I did not accept a beaker of white wine from the tank trailer parked right there in the street. He then charged me with Vietnam. I countered with the bitter Prague Spring of '68. He answered, then: "Why should we argue? Brezhnev, Johnson: they don't ask *us*. To Hell with them!"

That conversation took place in 1969. In 1991 I visited Kiev again with a group of Midwestern students who were studying Russian in Krasnodar. We put up in a hotel just off Kreshchatik, participated in a particularly fine tour of the Monastery of the Caves where the dryness and special soils have preserved many of Russia's first saints and historians, where one may actually see Nestor, first of the authors of the *Primary Chronicle*, the manuscript beginnings of Russian history. After our time underground, Diana and I and, by now, our children, Sarah and David, climbed the high bank of the Dnieper to look out across the river and east Kiev. We fell into conversation with two Russian mothers and their children, Kievans, who were, before school began, also spending a day sightseeing. As always, they were pleased and proud to hear our praises of their striking city, the high west bank looking off toward Asia, the monastery precincts, the bells which seemed, just then, to be tolling in their hundreds but afterwards, when we wished them good fortune, a shadow of sadness crossed their faces. They had lived here all their lives, including the time of the disaster at Chernobyl. They could not help but expect that tragedy to affect their children's genetic inheritance. "A beautiful city, yes, but not fortunate," said one of the mothers. Although there was, just then, no war, I remembered my plasterer's remark: "the *politikany* will not ask us."

As a weird American coda to this story, I should say that Diana is particularly thoughtful and careful of our health. When this 1991 chance to visit Kiev arose, she called our children's pediatrician in the States to ask if he thought the trip safe. As it turned out, he had recently died of AIDS. Then, a Russian friend told us that whatever the radiation dangers in Kiev, the chemical pollution of the air and water in Krasnodar, where we were then living, was the worst in Russia. At this point, Diana threw in the towel, and we all flew to Kiev in rickety World War II era planes with wooden propellers. So there!

After Kiev, it was time to depart for Lvov and the Polish border. This town, Lwiw in Polish, which was called Lemberg under the Austrians, is now Lvov and a Russian possession. Nearing the city, we passed under a formidable monument, right under, for the piece is a reinforced concrete reproduction of a peasant cart, a *tachanka*, mounting a machine gun and drawn by a *troika* of galloping Cossack horses. The horses loom over the road. Boris, one of our local Intourist guides, asked us to stop. We filed out and gathered at the foot of the monument.

"Do you know what this is?" Boris asked.

No one knew.

"It is a very important monument. It celebrates the victory of Budyonny's Second Cavalry Army over the Polish reactionaries who sought to take this land from Russia in 1918. Do you know who won that conflict?"

From the size and strenuous rush of the cart, anyone would assume that the Soviets had won, and we were, after all, still in the Union, but Boris surprised us.

"The Poles won! Stalin's pact with Hitler, just before the Great Fatherland War, World War II, got us this strip of Poland, not Budyonny's Cossacks. Then the Soviets put up this lying monument. Now, we can get back in the van."

"Boris," I asked, later. "Why did you tell us about the monument?"

"I'm not sure." he said, "but perhaps because I am a Jew, like Babel, who wrote so magnificently about Budyonny's cavalry, but was later forced to cultivate his famous 'genre of silence.' I am tired of silence."

The Polish border is the return to that Europe, of which Russia partakes only partially. Here the guards were always out-and-out nasty. Security? Jealousy? It seemed late for both. They brutally cut short our farewells with the Intourist guides who had become, by now, like blood kin. I watched a squinting blonde corporal read my letters from home, apparently checking my papers for Russian addresses, and saw these holy relics dropped, page by page, in the dust. It was my own fault. I saw that he couldn't read English and let this show.

Often, the gifts of Russian acquaintances, inveterate givers, were seized. Worst perhaps, for me, was the confiscation of a lovely old Pushkin. All decent souls will agree with the Russians, that poets make up, as Josif Brodsky wrote, the only genuine Central Committee. Pushkin and Shakespeare are co-chairs because they are able to present the harshest truth most gracefully and thus prove Keats no mere Romantic: beauty is truth, truth beauty. This bastard took my Pushkin!

The border sergeant leafed through the book, a parting gift from an old Moscow friend, a leather-bound edition.

"Contraband!" he said. "You may not take out."

"But it was a gift!"

"No matter. I keep."

"But why?"

The sergeant grinned. "I say contraband, but you speak Russian, I'll tell truth. My captain collects, reads poetry. I'll get, maybe, a day's leave for this. Anyway, old Pushkin mustn't leave Russia. We have only him, you know. Oh

Kay?" This last in English.

I said "Okay." As the poet said, in *Eugene Onegin*:

Habit is heaven's own redress;

It takes the place of happiness.

Border guards take. That's habit.

Then we crossed that last border, from Orthodox Russia to Catholic Poland. Okay. That ripoff, and my okay, left some of me on the Soviet, better, the Russian side of the border. Pushkin again, in *The Bronze Horseman*, explains my rather easy acquiescence:

The folk

Sees God's wrath and awaits punishment.

My "Okay" to the border guard placed me among this "folk," a little. There was nothing to be done. Further, most importantly, I *knew* thoroughly that this was the case and accepted it.

From the Soviet Union, from old Russia, from gray collective fields, we passed into Poland's green, private farms, free enterprise even then. The manager of the bank at the border could not give us Polish *zloty* for our dollars because the bank was closed. Okay, again? No. This smiling manager, said, "You've been in Poland before, you say and you can't find a way to exchange dollars? Legally, illegally, the first person you meet will buy enough of your dollars, and at double the official rate, to get you to the next bank, if you are foolish enough to go there," and he stepped outside his kiosk. He pulled *zloty* from three pockets. He bought, at the rate he had mentioned, one hundred dollars, enough to easily tide us over. In his lapel was, not Lenin but St. Christopher, patron of travelers, bridges, and possibilities. He testified to the *real* border.

But which side is *better?* That is harder to say.

CHAPTER VII
Stambul to Brussels, 1977

As Istanbul harbors Hagia Sophia, the Orthodox mother church, I include it in *Russia in Private*. I was standing in shifty Turkish gravel, a meter from dismemberment by Mercedes truck, bent to avoid the traffic's dusty gusts because I had been bewitched. The lovely and inexpensive day voyage up the Bosphorus had been my way of avoiding the clarion carpets of the Grand Bazaar. I enjoyed good fried fish served cheaply in newspaper and a fine cold Efes beer, even got a cheap haircut, $.50, in Garipce, "the town of vultures," and should have been sipping icy Chablis above Middle Eastern heat on the flight to Brussels and home. However, as I had an extra half hour until the little motor ship returned to Asiatic Stambul, I chose to ramble. A crooked oriental path beyond the pine tables of the fish shop ended with a bright, taut marquee tent displaying on its front panel a carpet - no, *the* carpet - deep scarlet, blue-black and blazing yellow diamond design. This was, clearly, the *objet* to make Wisconsin life complete.

The witch in question, a lovely lady from New Zealand, best buds with the Turkish banker who sold carpets here weekends "as a hobby," offered sweet coffee and compliments on my good taste. She managed to be both clipped and effective. I sloped back to my barge with a nicely packed $300 carpet under one arm (at that price they're not too large to carry,) and $39.00 in my wallet. Done! I had been.

This day on the water preceded a final student outing to St. Saviour in Chora - "in the fields" - a treasure of mosaics that translate very nearly the whole of the Bible for the illiterate and offer a suggestion of what Hagia Sophia might have been like before the activity of the iconoclasts and the coming of Islam. St. Saviour in Chora, by itself, could explain Russia's choice of Orthodoxy and yet the stiffness, the blazing coldness of these perfect tile structures was *not* Russian, not the flowing warmth of Rublyov's *Trinity*. No, the Slavs had added a soft grace of their own to this geometrical Greek perfection.

George the Indefatigable would take the troops to Troy that very night. I, after ten weeks of Slavic touring, was for Chicago and home. To conclude that plethora of hugs and blessings, which then dominated college farewells - *pace* the sixties - I leaned on a van to offer a passage from the *Iliad* which absolutely no one had requested and Shelby, that tour's clumsiest student, got my thumb with the door. "Sorry, *sorry*!!" and I had the bloodiest, plummiest, most purple thumb in Asia. As I waved farewell in agony, I became fully aware that I was broke, wounded, and alone in the mother city of Orthodoxy - and cursing most venially. Then, I took stock of my situation.

The purchase of that lovely carpet implied a bus trip to Brussels. I bought a bus ticket on my return from "the town of vultures" for $29.00. That left me ten. Because such discount buses ran illegally one met them clandestinely on busy, dusty road shoulders rather than at bus stations. Habitually early, my throng of one was only gradually augmented by Brussels-bound natives, young men and women and middle aged people traveling with whole families who were lucky enough to find work in northern Europe: the mines of Flanders in this case. This trip was necessary to support their bad habit of poverty and Turkishness, apparently. If I ever thought about it, my own Polish-German great-grandfather headed for Milwaukee by way of Hamburg - and certainly in steerage - in 1870.

To avoid, really, to respect the feeling of these many Turkish farewells, I thought of my last day in Istanbul. Mashed thumb wrapped in clotted red calico, I retrieved my one light bag, sleeping bag, briefcase and the carpet, of course, from the Hotel Shehir: cheap, friendly, and Kurdish (or "Mountain Turk" as the Turkish government liked to insist), bought *baklava* at a street stand, and spent a last hour at the small, frowsty zoo near Topkapi. The zoo offered a Turkish style Punch and Judy show, a lot of big birds, and a lion called Arslan. Arslan *means* lion, and C.S. Lewis knew that, too.

A word-lover, I'm utterly enthralled by such connections. Evening hours spent with my four now quite grown children reading the Inklings: Tolkien, Lewis, even Eddison's *The Worm Ouroboros*, until the kids revolted in their teens. The memory, here in a Turkish zoo, warmed me, even healed my thumb some. Then, it *was* time to trek to the sea road, slip aboard the black market bus, and here it came.

Mercedes, but no air. (The sea breeze had the consistency of warm gravy.) Overbooked by a dozen riders. One gentle driver tapped farewell couples and families. His partner, a beast-driver roared. Arslan? No, Arslan never roared. The bus got loaded with the aisle full of extras. I, the only apparent *giour*, unbeliever, was helped by acclamation, to a lovely window seat.

The steamy bus cabin provided a close-up of contemporary Turkey. Most passengers were slim, often balding, dark men in what was, given their choice of transportation, their one European suit. There were voluminous moms in head cloths, long sleeves, the traditional baggy pantaloons under capacious skirts next to their progeny in stone-washed jeans and Walkmans. A young bull, square-necked with arms like cornerposts, slid twinkling in beside me. His lunch filled a bulging camelbag made of a flatwoven *kilim*, but it dangled from that huge arm like a single worry bead. He greeted me in Vlaams, a cousin to my college German, so I knew that I was going to have communications.

Suddenly, we moved past bony donkeys, finned Buick taxis, porters with piano-sized boxes on their packsaddled spines, skinny boy-children rushing silver tripods of tiny coffee cups to important business deals: the everyday traffic of Istanbul. Wheel and foot gave us wide leeway in adobe-lined streets reminiscent of Wisconsin Sunday school illustrations. Pedestrians flattened against mud brick walls. Smaller vehicles climbed up on sidewalks. I grasped the reputation of pirate buses like mine. It was thirty-six hours to Brussels, and we were not starting off in any leisurely way.

Our overload was increased by one more stop in a northwest suburb when a short, worried man hammered at the bus door, while we stopped for an arterial. As the friendly driver was at the wheel, this pilgrim was let in, and immediately, he forced his way to the back of the bus, pried a teenybopper out of one of the six back seats, and sighed into place next to a large, traditional mom. The man then slid a lovely Circassian walnut stocked shotgun from a pantleg - barrels and then stock - and "Mom" at once stowed the armaments out of sight under a capacious skirt. "Trade goods" said my muscular seatmate. "Turkish lira aren't worth much in Brussels."

The trip itself: Sofia, Beograd and Munich, seemed, at the time, endless, given the heat, our crowding, and the returned thumb pangs. Again, it was, as flying is not, genuine travel, with time to reach beyond the nuclear self. My "bull" produced a two-liter canteen of gin and tonic, not being an observing Muslim, and described the life of Turkish miners in Flanders. He told of hard, punishing work, bent sideways to chip at a meter high coalface, no headroom, work so ghastly that Europeans didn't begrudge it. Still, it provided decent pay and a chance to really help the extended family at home in Ankara. Ahmad's father had been able to begin paying for a new Mercedes taxi with the Belgian revenue. My "bull" thought that most Turks would rather rise in, or return to, Turkey, if only they could guarantee their families some sort of an economic base there. "We Muslims don't plan to conquer half of Europe again," he grinned. "We don't care for the climate."

Conversation was limited to my miner, but there were other connections. Whenever the bus stopped, for gasoline or customs inspections at border crossings, the passengers, great lovers of soap and water and cleanliness, besieged whatever facilities were available. In Bulgaria and Yugoslavia the restrooms were unspeakable. This made arrival in southern Germany particularly grateful, but, as Ahmad explained, there existed one "problema."

The managers of the German rest stops tended to lock the toilets when a busload of Turks arrived, perhaps to avoid the trouble of cleaning up after them, perhaps out of sheer, mean racism. In any event, Ahmad had a plan. As a German-speaking American I could ask to use the facilities, and then my companions could hardly be kept from entering as well. This worked, even to the degree that the womens' restrooms were opened also, because, I imagine, the Germans were even more upset by the womens' use of the male facilities - that is, by disorder - than they were by the presence of the Turks. Afterwards, I was nicely rewarded with gin, baklava, and a ritual wipe with cologne whenever the shotgun packing supermom refreshed her own brood. When she did this in that stifling bus, the relief of cologne was considerable. She ritually said something that included the name of Allah, and I felt blessed.

Finally, near the end of our odyssey, one further "problema" developed. (The word brings a smile because that particular summer, "no problem," variously pronounced, was being stunningly over-used all through Eastern Europe. Once, when a disagreement developed between my students and a Turkish bartender, I ran into the logical extension of the idiom: not "no problem" but " PROBLEMA!," and very loud and clear, too.) Our "problema" here was this: behind and above that last row of six seats, and behind the family which provided cologne was a shelf-like platform where the off-duty driver rested. Though the beastly one of the two drivers dozed there at most for an hour at a stretch (the nice driver never used this couch.) The "beast" was adamant that none of the mere passengers pollute "his" space, though people were, as described, most uncomfortably quartered in the aisle. Twice, he ferociously drove a couple of the "mom's" younger children from the couch, and she, though formidable, could, apparently, not gainsay such an authoritative figure. Her husband, having gotten his contraband shotgun to the safety of her skirts, slept through everything, even the cologne baths. At the second such occurrence, on the Belgian border, my "bull" and I achieved a perfect, wordless understanding. It was the "beast's" habit, before he slept, to polish the toes of a handsome pair of tan Italian oxfords on the part of his trousers behind his knees before placing said shoes in the corner of his couch, like a monstrance on an altar. Three kilometers into Belgium, at his first snore, I whipped open my window, and the tan lovelies flew over my shoulder and into the Flemish night. Then, wordless, Ahmad and I shared a dreg of gin and tonic. Soon after this, my companion left the bus at a stop near his mine. He waved his clasped hands over his head to me before turning into the dark.

Brussels, on $9.15, was an anti-climax, almost. The brown beer was good, but scant, the French fries soggy. I couldn't afford a third course, and I found the subway to the airport with some difficulty. Nevertheless, it was a more than usually satisfying *cloture,* as we tend to say just now, when I rolled the utterly scarlet carpet, then my sleeping bag, out on the floor of the waiting room and dropped my head on my briefcase under the watchful eyes of the twin submachine-gunners who were a constant feature of Brussels airports that year after Lockerbie. I couldn't feel my mangled thumb at all. I left my boots on, but I went to sleep smiling

CHAPTER VIII

By Volga to Kizhi, 1997

She was called *Zosima Shazhkov* after a WW II naval hero, New Russia's attempt at a love boat. Still, no amount of manufactured fun could obscure the low, grassy Volga banks, white geese, goats, goatherds, occasional egrets, and even in August, the remains of the white nights. This summer sun was never long beneath that tawny, reed-rimmed horizon. Zosima, of course, was Dostoevsky's proto-saint, Alyesha Karamazov's beloved elder and teacher. He taught us, too.

We gathered in Chicago and Newark, former Slavic trippers and spouses, some who'd never made it to Russia, to re-enact for nine days, our Slavic department's old incursions on the bloc. Still, this was a new departure, for we were scheduled north out of Moscow, by water rather than road, and with Kizhi, that far, holy island, as our quite new goal. This pilgrimage was to oldest Russia, *Rus'*, the ancient forest citadel of Vikings and Slavs.

If it is for the twenty-two onion domes of Kizhi's pegged, pine Cathedral of Christ's Transfiguration that one travels, there are quicker routes. In St. Petersburg, one may board a hydrafoil and by river, canal, and Lake Onega "do" Kizhi and return to the northern Palmyra for a good restaurant dinner the same day. Still, that is not a pilgrimage, that is a "do." We traveled more slowly.

First, we flew to Prague. My seatmate, a specialist in laser physics teaching at a small New England school, was going home to Serbia for a visit. Serbia? Now? "Yes, and my name, God help me, is Voinichna: daughter of war." Then Voinichna, open, trusting, *Slavic*, dammit, began her chronicle. Sixty-student classes, two children, one of whom resembles Cupid but love, in her case, hasn't conquered all. Especially a drunken, redneck husband who, on principle, or out of inferiority, hates learning, hates books. (A major reason for this journey of Voinichna's is to rescue the best of the family library from threatened Beograd.)

How we do talk when we travel - freely, honestly - for we will never meet again. Voinichna's life was mothering, then, and research as she could. Add to that relentless reading: Vasco Popa - a Serb poet - Rebecca West's prophetic Yugoslavia book *Black Lamb and Grey Falcon* which, in 1941, foretold the fate of Serbia, Andrich's *Bridge on the Drina*, but also Blake, Beckett, Racine - for music, Richard Strauss's *Salome*. I'm glad I'm not that husband. Though Orthodox in her faith, she cannot agree with the forgiveness taught by Dostoevsky, is no subservient "*Russian* woman." Miriamne, what will become of you?

She departed the plane in Prague for a transfer to Beograd. What did she find there? What are such people to do in a murderous age? What they have always done, I expect. Comfort each other as they can and, reading relentlessly, go on with the "helping" work of parenting and teaching. There can never be too many parents and teachers. We may allow them their small vice of reading.

Our plane to Moscow was also Czech Airlines. However, here in the hinterland, old Aeroflot crates with few amenities were still in use. This was a fitting introduction. If the primitive, filthy plumbing bothered us, we'd have done better to go home at once. It didn't, and we did arrive at Vnukovo international airport outside Moscow. We were, of course, not met by the promised guide. Better and better; this *was* the Russia I knew. The lackadaisical passport and customs lines scared me momentarily, though. Too easy means nothing really seen or learned. However, we dragged our luggage through and around the dark and dusty airport for an hour, queued to change money, and then lacked the time to eat the lunches that we'd ordered. *This* Siberian tiger had not changed its stripes.

Finally, a substitute guide was found for us. Oksana had never traveled the Volga to Kizhi, knew little or nothing of that territory, but did speak decent English and, best of all, radiated the warmth and unstinting helpfulness which is the glory - and the willingly borne burden - of Russian women. She spoke a lovely, lilting poet's Russian. We were in good hands.

She began by finding a bus that would take us to the *Zosima Shazhkov*. Our ship was moored at the north edge of Moscow, in a canal that leads to the Volga. There were on board, as at the airport, no telephone tokens for those of our group who wished to assure relatives and children at home that our plane hadn't fallen from the skies. (It turned out, as usual, that a short conversation with a cleaning lady led to a laundry on the pier that, illogically, could supply tokens. Our first hurdle was surmounted.)

The *Zosima* herself, though she quickly came to feel like home, began also as a mixed blessing. A folk orchestra, fully costumed, piped each arriving voyager aboard. This was utterly embarrassing. However, the cabins were "modern" and comfortable, though the shower wet down the whole bathroom and, unlike the tales of Gogol, there were no cockroaches "as big as prunes" to witness one's ablutions. Then, to replace the light lunches we were forced to leave standing at the airport, there was a tasty, elegantly served Russian dinner, and we found ourselves seated with an attractive group of travelers from Holland. They possessed the usual, no, really quite unusual in this century, quiet, civilized, Dutch humor and forbearance. There were, also, Italians, who turned out to be all tenors, and a group of second generation *emigré* Russians from Australia. These last were the children of intellectuals and bourgeois who fled to China during the revolution and the civil war which followed. The second generation moved on to Australia, trained as engineers, lawyers - professionals - but took good care that their children preserved the Russian language, the heart of the culture. For these travelers, this was a first sight of the distant motherland - *rodina* - richest of Russian nouns and concepts. It was an odd feeling to explain Russian matters to them. I knew the terrain better, but only the terrain. *They* knew Russia better, through the humming of their blood, the cradlesongs of their Russian mothers.

We passengers shaped up as a sartorially not too demanding group. Further, everyone was quite pleased with the German-built ship, which meant that everyone was in a good mood. As on other cruises, on the Black

Sea, some international naval etiquette seems to leave Russian anarchy at the water's edge. (How difficult I am to please. I come to this country in large part for its holy spirit and liberating indifference to mundane order, but immediately rejoice in clean towels and hot water on a German boat. How *does* one spell "hypocrite"?)

We were to tour Moscow for two days before splashing north toward Kizhi and, ultimately, St. Petersburg. Vassily the Blessed's barbershop stripes in the corner of rosy Red Square never come amiss, because of their multicolored statement that a church needn't be gray, square, and cold. The warm brick of the Kremlin sends a subliminal welcome, surrounds mainly, for me, the square church-caskets that enclose the jeweled icons of Rublyov and Feofan Grek. Especially, the many sparkling, gilded domes, one onion shape, and the crooked crosses surmounting crescent moons that embellish them are part and parcel of this very Slavic, gross and irrational treasure. No, this is not the West.

An excursion to the New Virgin Monastery in south Moscow provided warm pink brick, famous graves, and a cubical stone cathedral. Such churches, microcosms of the universe for the faithful, made up now, as thirty-six years ago in 1961, the bulk of anyone's Russian souvenir photographs. One reflected again upon the vanity of socialism's fruitless attempt to rationalize this life, to put flesh on Rousseau's and Marx's dreams of universal love. These churches, these old depositories of beauty, as of all the world's suffering, continue to shield candles burned before the icons that both embody and promise a better, otherworldly future. In Russia now, as during the Soviet three-score and ten, the cobbled floors of these refuges receive the pious kisses of strong women fighting overwork and despair. The gilded beauty of the *iconostas*, the icon screen, is perhaps a more fitting witness to grief than the psychiatrist's genuine leather armchair, or the aluminum cabin of a Czech plane.

On the evening of this first day in Moscow, I was invited to a former student's birthday party. The party, his thirtieth, and therefore ominous, occurred at his suburban Moscow *dacha*. Jeremy, who was in business in Russia, promised to address my group on the commercial practices of the burgeoning Russian free market, but he never found the time. As I had been unable to find him at any of his three telephone numbers, I assumed that he was too busy just then to instruct us. However, I found a note from him when we returned to the *Zosima* from our day's tour of Moscow: "I'll have you picked up at eight."

At 11:30 p.m., a dusty black Volvo arrived to take me to Jeremy's party. The shoulder holsters of Jeremy's "associates" were visible, on the lighted dock, to members of my group quietly enjoying a glass of white wine on the upper deck. As these emissaries had another former student, Lynn, with them to identify me, I returned her big hug and missed the shoulder holsters. I boarded the Volvo talking, as is my wont, when I should have been observing.

Two hours, one of which was spent in an amateur auto repair shop, and fifty kilometers later, it developed that Jeremy was already sleeping off the effects of his blast at the *dacha*. (This information I gleaned from a carload of Englishmen met on Jeremy's five kilometer driveway. As Lynn needed to arrive at her desk at six the next morning, she told me to "be careful" and accepted a ride back to Moscow offered by the Englishmen.) When we arrived at Jeremy's place, it was soon clear that Lynn had been percipient, I had been stupid. It took several buckets of water to arouse Jeremy enough to attack me for my lateness, though repairs on the much misused Volvo had certainly lengthened the evening and, in any event, my arrival had been altogether arranged by Jeremy. Other "associates," snappily dressed like all *new Russians,* wives rather dripping with jewelry, and Jeremy's wife, along with a visiting mother from Grosse Pointe and Jeremy's mother-in-law, were spiritedly finishing off the *shishkebab,* herring, and pepper vodka which remained from the feast. At least, my former student's two young daughters were sensibly in bed, asleep.

I weathered a tide of Jeremy's profanity because I did need his car and at least one associate to make it back to Moscow. I drank a congratulatory glass of the pepper vodka, then switched to lemonade. This looked like a good party to miss. The *dacha,* brought in sections from Finland, was of lovely clear pine, furnished modern Scandinavian, except for purchased moose and boar heads. The conversation, though in Russian, was also international. This conversation had everything to do with the consumption of German automobiles and French perfume and nothing to do with business. When I, foolishly, asked about *that,* I got one cold, greasy monosyllable: *neft.* Crude oil. I grasped, rather rapidly, that this business was not up for discussion.

My arrival was apparently the signal for the departure of the associates and their wives. A new guest, however, the next-door neighbor, did drop in "to drink with the American." Unfortunately, he didn't mean Jeremy. When I declined a drink with him, neither of us absolutely needed a 3 a.m. vodka, this neighbor drank his glass and mine, told me that he couldn't stand Americans, that my Russian was too primitive for me to have been Jeremy's teacher, and that he could beat me at arm wrestling. Such rudeness is utterly uncommon in my experience of Russia, if central to the new manners of the *krutiye* or "new Russians." I refused the match. The neighbor embraced me, rubbed a wire-whiskered chin against my shrinking neck, and we were enveloped in the CO fumes of the rapidly departing "associates." Jeremy alone sat across the Finnish picnic table from the neighbor and me and watched, glassy-eyed. He certainly said nothing to intervene with this odd type. I looked to Jeremy's bodyguards, but as they had been standing with a couple of bottles near the villa, they now subsided into recumbent heaps. My promised early ride to Moscow looked pretty iffy. Our *troika* was left to celebrate alone.

"I don't like professors," said the neighbor, *apropos* of nothing that I had said or done, unless he was angered because I had done or said nothing. "You think you're too good for us Mafiosi. Let me tell you, we know how to enjoy ourselves! *Nam veselo!*" His too stereotypical bull neck swelled in his black mock turtleneck. "Why in Hell Dcheremy invite if won't drink, afraid fight?" I got up and said that I would walk back to Moscow rather than continue so. Jeremy's eyes widened, but he still said nothing. At this juncture, the Grosse Pointe mother appeared to take me into the *dacha* as the neighbor left, cursing, with my cigarette lighter in his pocket. Mrs. Pocock, the mother, intimated that it would be wise if I slept in her room now. Upstairs, she pointed out a corner with a sleeping bag, then locked me in the room. I plopped down on the bag but found it hard to sleep. After that lengthy, timeless interval needed by an adrenalin-suffused organism to attain sleep, I began to lose consciousness in snatches, then was quite roused by the sound of shots. They seemed to come from the neighbor's direction, to "thwack" into the *dacha's* pine. I was done sleeping. However, there were no more shots.

Early in the morning, the door now unlocked, I descended through the sleeping dacha, past the snoring bodyguards, to find a happy party of stray dogs finishing off the feast. I had easily two hours to ruminate before the heaped body-guard-chauffeurs began to twitch. Once they were up, it appeared that we needed to re-attach the muffler lost on the driveway and arrange to drag a new Mercedes, which had lost more than a muffler. The long driveway, assembled of cement plates "organized" and brought from a nearby abandoned airfield and tipped crazily by winter frosts, was mere murder for foreign cars. (Russian automobiles are built with more clearance, and for good reason.) Jeremy appeared to kiss me on both cheeks. I avoided the third kiss, on the mouth, for good and sufficient reasons. Then, I endured two hours of the chauffeur's hypocritical praise of Jeremy before I was dropped at the *Zosima*. Of course, I'd missed the Kremlin tour with my small group. They, missing Jeremy's feast, hadn't missed a thing.

Good people that they were, my abandoned charges had gone right ahead to enjoy their Kremlin. Oksana and a local guide had done a fine job of the churches and the armory, and I was not aware of a single accusatory glance. So much for Russo-American "beeznees."

Though this second Moscow afternoon was billed as free time, I offered a tour of the Tretyakovsky Gallery to make up for my disappearance. Russians, always fond of the diminutive, call it "Tretyakovka." I got several takers. The clean, efficient metro took us there easily and, for a wonder, there were few other visitors. Clinging wisps of Mafia were dissolved at once by my favorite, quiet spring landscape, Savrasov's *The Blackbirds Have Arrived* with its aspens, thawing snow and, almost, the melodious chiming of European blackbirds behind a village church with its tent-shaped gray *shatyor* steeple. Then Levitan's *Above Eternal Peace*, a landscape twelve feet square, in blues, grays, and a bit of green. It depicts a tiny still island, with the cube of a church, and before both, stretching out and ahead for miles, a great swelling tract of the Volga. The piece literally pacifies, and I found myself before it three separate times that one afternoon. In a further hall of this, the greatest repository of Russian paintings, the modernist Vrubel's *Demon*, based on a poem of Lermontov, lies, a fallen angel, like Russia, all in ruins. Here, in Moscow, relatively neat, spruced up and murderous, Vrubel's symbolic ruin lay all about us. Levitan's quiet islands and churches are what we will encounter to the north. Here there are, though, harbingers: the fine icon collection. There is Rublyev's half worn away, stern, handsome head of Christ on linden wood and, most essential, that same artist's *Trinity*, a depiction of the three angels who dined with Abraham under the oak at Mamre, promised him a son, Isaac, and the triumph of Israel. For Russians, now, and perhaps earlier, the icon also represents Yaroslav's gathering together of the *Rus* lands, the unification of an earlier, and, now, again disunited, chaotic Russia. The calm, serenely assured faces of the angels, who are also the Trinity, promise peace. So utterly convincing are they that one can accept, for the time, the promise.

After this much aesthetic intensity, Homer's "brazen belly" began to call. The Moscow streets awaited us with a Russian version of McDonald's, "Russian Bistro." (Russian rumor, which would appropriate the Grand Canyon for Slavia, asserts that "bistro" is a corruption of the Russian "quick!," *bystra!* The cossacks in Paris after Napoleon's defeat in 1812 are said to have taught the word to Parisian bartenders. "Russian Bistro" was a fairly new chain. *Pirozhki,* meat-filled personal pies, and, if you like, cognac, fill the place of burgers and Coke. Dessert was a large, dried-apricot tart but the so-called *borshcht* was a tasteless red bouillon, and the pastry was made and frozen elsewhere. The pure plastic essence of American fast food had been sedulously monkeyed with. Luckily, we still had time to catch a genuine Russian dinner on the *Zosima.*

Moscow, then, prepared us for holy *Rus* with the Kremlin's stone, brick, and plaster cathedrals, though real Russia was *kondovaya,* close-grained, durable spruce. The rich icon hoard of the *Tretyakovka* had given us further intimations of old Russia. Still, these solid *things,* traditional value markers, threaten to become mere museum pieces, irrelevant before the spectacle of Pizza Hut, McDonald's, Lancôme, Mercedes Moscow, and Russian Bistro. Citizens, ourselves, of just such a paradise, we embarked without regret for the north and whatever might remain of an older *Rus.*

We were conveyed by *Zosima Shazhkov* from Moscow, by canal and lock to and along the Volga, then on other canals, lakes, and tributary streams. We traveled for nine days. On the way, like the stations of a crooked Orthodox cross, we stopped at Uglich, Yaroslavl, Goritsy, Kizhi, Svirstroy, and Valaam, before arriving in St. Petersburg. We were giving ourselves the now rare luxury of time to feel and imagine. Like Chaucer's pilgrims and with equal levity, we told and listened to each other's stories while underway. We were neither bored nor, I hope, ultimately disappointed by our pilgrimage route or ourselves, though the gray granite of the Baltic shield allows Kizhi and Valaam no golden sands and the sun, even that close to Midsummer's Day, did not warm us out of our windbreakers. The charms of this northernmost Russia are modest and retiring, but they find their mark in the heart. The looming firs, hemlock, and spruce form the horizon and are also the matter from which this northern civilization was, and to a degree still is, made.

That first evening out of Moscow, we passed between four absolutely hieratic images of robust, gigantic Soviet laborers, male and female. They are formed of the same cement and steel reinforcing rods that wall the twenty some locks of the canals which now, with the Volga, Svir and Neva rivers, join Moscow and St. Petersburg. Much of the canal building was done by political prisoners in Stalin's time. Peter the Great had, indeed, forced the building of St. Petersburg in much the same way two hundred years earlier, except that he used serfs. These present, oddly *Egyptian* figures mark the entrance to the canal that leads to the Volga. Now the system that murdered their models has been changed for the better. Still, the figures stand, idealized workers, ominously glorious after long, systematic betrayal.

Each day of our journey centered on another historic settlement. The first, Uglich, is one of the "Golden Ring" of princely seats that circle Moscow. Here Boris Godunov is said to have instigated the murder of the child-tsar Dimitry, the last of the founding dynasty of Rurik, in the sixteenth century. Dimitry dead, however, led to "The Time of the Troubles," thirty years of virtual anarchy when a series of Pretenders supported by Polish arms and ambitious Russian boyars vied to rule Russia. Ultimately, continual disorder became so unbearable that the Russian nobility was able to unite on the choice of the first Romanov tsar. The Romanovs, of course, ruled until the 1917 Revolution. The Time of the Troubles, though, *Smutnye vremena*, seems at least partially paralleled by the present gangster state of Russia.

In the walls of the Cathedral at Uglich are said to be buried clay pots, which give the Orthodox chants a special, echoing richness. Did they similarly amplify the cries of the stabbed child, Dimitry, or did the boy, like Boris and Gleb, the most popular because "kenotic" saints of old Russia, accept his death unresisting? Here, a quotation seems to help:

Saints Boris and Gleb created in Russia a particular...order of "sufferers," the most paradoxical order of Russian saints. In it are included some victims of political crimes among the princes or simply victims of a violent death. Among them one finds many infants, the most famous, Prince Demetrius of Uglich in the sixteenth century, in whom the idea of an innocent death is blended with the idea of purity. In most cases it is difficult to speak of voluntary death; one is entitled to speak only of nonresistance to death. Apparently, this nonresistance communicates the quality of voluntary sacrifice to death by violence and purifies the victim in those cases where, except for infants, the natural conditions of purity are lacking.

G.P. Fedotov, *The Russian Religious Mind*. Harper Torchbook. 1960.

***

Basic to this sanctity is the idea of *kenosis*, meaning that Christ renounced His divine nature in Incarnation. He could, therefore, experience human suffering at the time of the Passion. This is the same root as stradanie (suffering). "Sufferers," in Fedotov's sense, imitate Christ in their deaths. Dimitry of Uglich is celebrated as one of these. Nonresistance, the acceptance of suffering, is and has been, in Russia, not a political ploy but an end in itself. (It is no accident, I think, that the peasant word for the almost superhuman labor of harvest was *strada*, passion.) People in such a tradition can hardly be expected to concern themselves with problem solving. Of course, some Russians no longer accept this tradition. Peter the Great never did.

Dimitry was hardly the only sufferer here. Uglich was *serially* destroyed by the Tatars, by Polish invaders during that same Time of the Troubles (the Poles slaughtered a thousand inhabitants who had taken refuge in the cathedral) and by the Russians in repeated internecine conflicts. There was, as always here, plenty of suffering to go round.

The main Uglich church is the Cathedral of the Transfiguration of the Savior. Indeed, "Transfiguration" is a favorite church name here in the north, with its intimations of an ultimate freedom from the flesh, an ultimate spiritualization. Perhaps, this is because, even in Russia, there is a limit to fleshly suffering. It may be that one lives nearer this limit in the relatively desert north. In any event, Uglich's "Transfiguration" possesses a six-tiered icon screen and fifty murals of scenes from the Old and New Testaments.

In an illiterate age, which, in Russia, lasted until well after 1917, these walls *were* the Bible. The church, like every Orthodox church, was a microcosm, a small universe, with Christ the Ultimate Judge frowning down from the half-sphere of the main dome. However, as in our universe, the church *was* tied to the necessities of this world as well. The Feast of the Transfiguration on August 19 is also the time of the sanctification of summer apples. Only after this date ought they to be picked and eaten.

Yaroslavl, our next port of call, is the place where young Yaroslav, not yet "the Wise," not yet ruler of Kievan *Rus*, not until later lawgiver in a country devoid of fixed law, is said to have fought a bear, axe to claw. Then, he founded Yaroslavl on the spot. True or not, this seems an honest parable. Just so are men matured and civilizations founded, by killing the bear.

On the dock a jazz band: string bass, cornet, trombone, clarinet, drum, and balalaika played *Muskrat Ramble*, *When You're Smilin'*, *Strangers in the Night*, *When the Saints...* and, last, *Moscow Nights*. Three bandsmen were gray-headed and three were not. They had just the right grasp and attitude for our mixed group and for the music. What magnificent buskers they were, though the horns were dented and old and the drum patched. One contributes so very gladly - to one's own culture? Whose? It's a pain to be a liberal, no wonder we dwindle. Back to Yaroslavl.

The guide's English was excellent, though she did rather often flute: "our beautiful city." Nevertheless, she knew her trade, her history. Catherine the Great beautified this neglected center some thousand years after Yaroslav had gone on to unify, codify Kievan *Rus*. Her son Paul, kept too long in leading strings, did his best to nullify her efforts with the nasty, yellow-stucco institutional structures that deface most Russian, and, for that matter, most Eastern European governmental centers. One wonders if tastelessness was the political virtue in the eighteenth century. Yaroslavl's Red Square has the Prophet Elijah as its centerpiece, since 1645. A good Lenin, copied from the one at St. Petersburg's Finland Station, contents himself with a secondary square. I am a great fan of such small, puzzling contradictions.

There is, of course, a cathedral. This one has an elaborate, bloody Last Judgment, where only "Germans" (*nemtsy*, the Russian word for all foreigners) are damned, pitch-forked by muscular demons into the maw of the Great Serpent, while the Orthodox rise to glory. To a "German" in good standing, this becomes a bit wearing.

At the sixteenth century Savior-Transfiguration monastery, a bell-ringer works a collection of bells preserved from the abandoned small churches of the villages round about. An adroit puppet-master, his silvery peals, alarums and calls to grief and prayer, cascade and wash me happily back in time. In Mrs. Bloom's house, where I lived in the Wisconsin village of Genesee, just such a tenor bell marked my steps to Sunday school and church. That the bell ringer now hawks tapes of his music can hardly offend; how is he otherwise to live in a land without Grand Prince Yaroslav's once pristine order? Another peddler, this one of the ubiquitous *matrëshka* nesting dolls, shows us a traveler's check which a crafty tourist has signed in neither place. Still, he laughs, and says, "You Germans are learning our Russia too quickly." Not only a bell ringer, even a skillful conman deserves some applause.

We walk, finally, down a broad pedestrian boulevard, well-planted and quite unlittered, to the juncture of Yaroslavl's two rivers, to "Bear Corner," where the prince fought and killed his beast. On the way we pass a recent sculpture based upon Rublyev's *Trinity* icon. Leaving aside for the moment the question of whether an icon ought to be rendered in another medium, for original icons are said to be the work, through a painter or *ikonopisets*, of God, the image of the three angels together at Abraham's table has come, traditionally, to stand for unity. Of course: three is one, and one is three. The point here, however, is that *Trinity* is, especially, Yaroslav's icon, because he was able, for a time, to bring that unity to *Rus* which could it have been prolonged might have kept the land free of the Tatar-Mongol yoke and kept Russia European. How easily and quickly the spiritual becomes historical, the historical spiritual. Yaroslav "gathered the lands," for about the length of our whole American history, around Kiev's authority. Long for us, a mere breathing space for a country with a twelve-hundred year history.

As we return to the ship, we must pace the long gauntlet of amateur merchants. We realize that even Russians can't eat Adam Smith's theory, unbuttered history. The jazz combo plays us away with *"When the saints. . ."*.

Always, we gravitate north. A baroque bell tower projecting above the surface of a vast Soviet reservoir marks the sunken village of Kalazin. At the same time, that tower says something weighty, terrible, about history. What waters will cover *us*?

Then, at Goritsy on the White Lake, we visit a monastery once made rich by the guilt and gifts of Ivan the Terrible. Our local guide informs us that Ivan had bad press and was really rather nice. She goes on to make this news relevant. In the town of Goritsy, the former Party chairman is now president of the bank. "He's still beloved of the people," she says with an irony that must sink right to the bottom of the White Lake. "So, you see," she adds, innocently, "how first impressions may lead one astray. Our former Chairman and Ivan the Terrible were like peas in a pod."

This monastery, it appears, is undergoing renewal. There is no capital to help them at the moment, but twelve monks are on their way here to attempt to resuscitate the buildings. This is a fortress enclosure built for a hundred monks and five hundred soldiers in the sixteenth century. Nevertheless, I envy those monks. They will cultivate the fields within and without the walls, they will see the faded, gorgeous murals of the Great Gate setting forth their unworldly Christian values for the literate and illiterate alike. Christ, His Mother, and His Saints stand here robed in sun- and frost-faded saffron, pinks, and ice blues, their faces warm and serene. The monks will pace their day to the monastery bells' matins and compline, and these are sounding now, even before their arrival, as if to entice them. The bell tones are warm and low. Why, one might just live here! The Queen Anne's Lace, wild chicory, even the burdock are all native at home, as is this particular slant of clean northern light, a painter's, no, an *ikonopisets's* light, which turns this old stone, that old wood, rosy. However, it *is* difficult for an agnostic to become a monk.

Perhaps it was the long line of Russians selling peasant shirts, linoleum prints, and carved bears; but also a pitiful handful of used books, wildflowers (*lyesniye mariki*), and blackberries by the glassful. It may have been the unkempt, long grass look of the churchyards. (We insist on graves well clipped. I wonder what that costs us, even monetarily.) It was certainly the creature comfort of *Zosima*, the white wine sundowner on the deck as contrasted with the utterly temporary look of Russian life. They all led to the deck chair topic, "Russia, now."

Alex from Sidney, born of Russian parents in Harbin, Manchuria, during the Russian Civil War, now a retired engineer: "I can't believe that Russians could have worked so *badly* with concrete and reinforcing rods. The canals and locks are positively unsafe." Xenia, the wife of a Russian Australian lawyer, quoted an uncle seen for the first time the day before near Yaroslavl: "Seventy years the Bolsheviks taught us, and we're still in first grade." *"Myetka!"* crows Alex, "The old man is right on." Alex is pleased to find Russians still ready-tongued. He does not attack his roots gladly.

The decay of cement apartment houses and pavements, the proliferation of this private "trade" that was little removed from begging, and the somehow shameful public ruin of this onetime super power struck us all. Old enough to have experienced nuclear attack drills, cowering and giggling under wooden tables in school basements, to have admired Gagarin on the first space mission, we too wanted to know *Who is to Blame?* and *What is to Be Done?* These are the oldest questions in Russian history, it seems, the titles of half of the books of the nineteenth century. Who, what indeed?

Deborah alone, a Seattle musician, artist, mom, said, in a half-whisper - she's no orator - "I would approach this differently. Forty magnificent churches certainly outweigh the absence of lawnmowers. Think of the voices of that group in the Uglich cathedral, *The Ark*, (especially the counter tenor) could straighten the hair on the back of one's neck. The exactness of that old uncle's remark about first grade, even, his *myetkost* (Deb was a Russian student years ago). Something is *right* here, too. When we can sing like that, then, maybe, we can criticize. It is for us to learn, as well as for them, I think. We must help these awful peddlers, but they... but they have a word to say, too, something to contribute. I feel, seeing the big bad bear in agony, as if I have been in first grade for thirty years myself." This was said, as I noted, *sotto voce*. It was not the speech my clumsy academese has made it here. It led to an evening of comparative culture and comparative lives.

We spoke of malls and *souks*, for Deb had done Peace Corps work in Tunisia, the cry of the muezzin and the bellow of the born-again. Our kids' pictures came out, of course. How were *they* to live? Did the "free market" suffice as theology? Did we know "Who?" and "What?" It may be that liberalism occasionally does something besides dithering and dwindling. "What is to be done?" is an open question, not to be answered, one felt this everywhere, with our easy "work, save, invest," any more than with Marx's theses. Though the beast Poverty haunted poor, and extremely rich, Russia, so did Beauty. The Orthodox hymns in Uglich: "We wish you many years... ." "The Evil One prowls like a raging lion... ." a sevenfold Amen, and the fantastic majolica tiles on the red brick churches of Yaroslavl, built by merchant families that traded along the old silk route, the fine, fading murals of Goritsy, was there some answer beyond the "free market" here?

A stiff north wind buffeted *Zosima* all night as we crossed 140 miles of

Lake Onega to, finally, Kizhi. Then, at dawn, we passed brushy skerries and saw, straight ahead, the Cathedral of Christ's Transfiguration Kizhi.

Is it the cold, the sharp and surprising seasonal changes, or the northern love of the magical, the Laplander in all evergreen addicts that makes just "transfiguration" the major church name here? The hundred-foot cone decorated with silvery bells, onion domes, seemed, indeed, a transfigured pine, the domes; pine cones. The spruce of the log frame, the aspen of the fish-scale shingles, showed pewter-silver and silver-blue in dawn light. The late-August day, almost October, near this beauty was certainly a serendipitous gift.

Kizhi is an old Finno-Ugric word meaning "the place of the games," perhaps something like Odysseus' Phaiakia. In the north of Russia, and, indeed, in Central Russia, too, there is more than a trace of Viking and Finnish blood and culture, perhaps a stiffening of the endemic Slavic softness.

There are few trees here on the island. Winter is cold and the island tiny. Firewood must be brought by boat. As frequent tourist hydrofoils do arrive by way of the canals and the river Svir, barns, chapels, cabins and mills, examples of northern spruce architecture, have been brought (as if the cathedral weren't sufficient) to make of Kizhi a museum island. I use the word "spruce," a close-grained conifer, but my dictionary says "deal," and then goes on to describe that wood as seven to nine inches wide, six feet long, not over three inches thick and sawed from fir or pine. Once, though, this was the administrative center for 130 villages, the cathedral porch its parliament. Yes, parliament, a strange word in Russia, fits too. Like the Scandinavian "Ting," the "Vesch"' ruled Novgorod, and Onega and environs were one of the five parts of Lord Great Novgorod's domain. Novgorod's senate of merchants set the example for democratic rule in that city's possessions as well. Then, with Moscow's seizure of Novgorod, according to Tatyana Tolstaya, the now-reigning Tolstoy, civilization was crushed along with democracy, and the well-shod, literate citizens of Novgorod became, again, barefoot and ignorant.

Besides the influence of Novgorod, Kizhi is one of those distant corners, distant, that is, from Moscow, to which, after the seventeenth century church reforms of the Patriarch Nikon, the Old Believers, those who rejected these reforms, fled. Often merchants, literate like Luther's Protestants, these refugees certainly played a role in the creative culture and beauty of Kizhi as well. To give one formalistic example, Nikon forbade the use of the tent or *shatyor* form in the roofing of churches, insisted upon the onion dome. "Christ's Transfiguration" is all domes, but arranged in "shatyor," tent or cone, shape and that's how these "protestants" skinned *that* cat.

Kizhi, and the North around it, are both an official museum and the preservation of the oldest Russia, Kievan Rus. The wood structure which once graced all Russia, but also the oral epics of Vladimir's banquet hall, the *byliny*, were preserved in memory here until well into the 1920's. Here a Slavic parallel to the western "Matter of Britain," the King Arthur tales, was kept in mind. Here in the North, where the Mongols never penetrated, where, perhaps because of the influence of Novgorod, true serfdom, *barshchina*, labor for one's lord, never took root, there was what my otherwise pious Soviet source, A.V. Opolovnikov's *Kizhi* calls *"the furious preference for images and forms of old Russian culture."* *Furious.* Yes, exactly so. Here the Old Believers, along with runaway prisoners and escaped serfs and Finnish fishermen, fought the long defeat and defended their preference for local authority as long as possible. In the *gubnaya izba*, the "lip hut," this part of what was once Novgorod's Onega "fifth" governed. In the cathedral, they were slaughtered by Hetman Sapieha's Poles in the time of the troubles after the child Dimitry's, and then his slayer Godunov's, death. In 1648, they beat a state judge who oppressed them. Here, in 1649, the local peasants were called to be "plow soldiers" by Aleksey Mixailovich, the second Romanov tsar, hoping to fend off further such incursions at little expense, here in 1658 the locals sent a plea called a "forehead beating" to that same Aleksey, announcing, not too submissively, that if farming, soldiering, and taxes killed them all, there would be no one to defend the land when the "Germans" came. In 1695, the local inhabitants assembled with oaken clubs and spears before the cathedral and declared a strike against the iron works. In 1769, Catherine the Great felt moved to send artillery to this same church, open fire on workers striking against the same iron works and brand and exile the leaders. Kizhi's history then is intimately bound up with the Cathedral of the Transfiguration, but not, mostly, with *this* building.

After Sapieha's slaughter there of the inhabitants during the Time of the Troubles, the then cathedral - a "summer" church in any event, used for great holidays but too cold in the winter months - was largely abandoned for its nearby "winter" partner, the Church of the Intercession. Here again,

I think, that "furious" love of old Russian imagery is apparent. Intercession is a translation for "shroud." It implies, however, not death but the Virgin's protection. Not the miracle of the transfiguration in this case, but the perhaps more useful magic of safety, for a while. The present, striking, silvery spire, said to have been sketched out in a few moments by Peter I, Peter the Great himself, was built in 1714. Another, somehow more likely story, refers to a "Master Nestor" who, having completed the church, said "The like of this church has not been, isn't, won't be," and threw his axe far out into Lake Onega. But this, too, is legend, for there is an earlier church nearby that has much in common with "Transfiguration." The church derives, grows out of, past models, as we do.

Here, though I have criticized my source, I should like to quote his description of Kizhi's chief beauty:

Cupolas, cupolas...twenty-two. They aim their wings...in all directions, like the kokoshniki [elaborate, embroidered linen tiaras] of Russian beauties. And on their peaks, well-formed drums and onion-shaped domes with crosses scaled with silvery aspen. In the northern white nights they gleam with an almost phosphorescent glow; at sunset, when the sun slowly and majestically slips into the waters of the lake, they glisten with a tremulous purple. Now they show blue, reflecting the firmament, now dim, leaden, now moss green or brown, earthen. One ring, a second, a third and fourth...Ever higher, and the main dome has penetrated the sky itself, crowning the whole grand thirty-seven meter pyramid. [Opolovnikov, A.V., Kizhi. Pamyatniki Zodchestva. Izdatel'stvo Literatury po Stroitel'stvy Moskva - 1970.] (My translation.)

***

Kizhi is a small island. It is two hundred to six hundred yards wide and three miles long. Still, Transfiguration Cathedral is not the island's only attraction. We followed our good guide, saw barn mows furnished with plows, and drags and horse harness not utterly foreign to a boy raised on a sixty-acre Wisconsin farm in the '30s and '40s. Indeed, one lovely surprise was the essentially international quality of many tools now used, even homemade ones. Of course, my ancestors were Polish potato farmers not all that far from Kizhi. Nevertheless, a windmill, the turning of grindstones by wind power, was new to me, for our mill in Genesee was powered by water from a millrace turning a water wheel. Everywhere "deal," the close-grained fir and spruce, softened, warmed the view.

Finally, we came to a small chapel, no more than twelve feet high and were asked to wait a moment. It was just time for the *zvonar'*, the deacon to come ring compline, *completa hora*, evening prayers. Soft, light, falling on the bare, beaten path, long grass and foxtail, the notes seemed cool, hot, silvery-fine, and weighty as mercury. The setting sun turned the chapel's one dome and the cathedral's many, mauve then purple. I remembered the words of a woodcarver whom we met earlier in a museum craft shop, which in other places would have offered pickled folk art. This carver displayed a variety of birch drinking vessels. Karelia is not far and is famous for bird's-eye birch. Here were cups, plates, mugs of this material, and one great *kovsh*, in Scotland *cuach*, and I would give much to know the connection. This is a drinking bowl, often formed with the head and tail of a duck for handles, for the duck is a bird that stands for plenty. This piece, perhaps eight inches across, was lovely in shape and finish because of the natural freckling given the breast by the quarter-sawed bird's-eye. I asked the price, politely, but he smiled and said that he was a "maker" not a "peddler," and these pieces were meant for a display in St. Petersburg. "*Kakaya krasota,*" ("what beauty") said one of my former students. "Of course," said the carver. "We could not live here, in the dark of the far North, without beauty." Now, the silvery, mercurial notes falling on my suddenly naked self were as light, as heavy, as unearned, as joyous, as beauty itself, as the sudden last ray of the red sun.

It was not easy to leave Kizhi.

CHAPTER VIII

The Red Goddess in Krasnodar, 1991

The title, remodeled from Robert Graves, is meant to suggest the beauty of character of women in Russia. The primary meaning of "red" in that country is not political. Red Square, named centuries before the Communists, means "Beautiful Square." Like Graves' Mediterranean fates and goddesses, the *parki* or fates of Krasnodar, our station in southern Russia, are feminine. The "free market" is a distant dream, and an American dream at that. "Putin cannot help," is the joke that replaces the Yeltsin joke in people's mouths. Survival depends largely upon women's labor and women's wit.

Russia's favorite poet is Alexander Sergeyevich Pushkin. Late in his short life, after many works and many loves, he wrote:

> *Now my desire's a quiet life*
>
> *And my ideal a plain housewife,*
>
> *Self-government and cabbage soup.*

This kind of existence he called, elsewhere:

> *The women's prattle of the fates,*
>
> *The sleepy trembling of the night:*
>
> *The mousey scurrying of life.*

Pushkin was, no doubt, a male chauvinist pig, a user of women who, when tired, expected to be coddled by those he had used. Russia, I think, is like this now. I realize that after a plethora of first-hand reports, enough would seem to have been written about that part of the world. Nevertheless, an attempt is made here to redress what Rebecca West once called "the male defect...lunacy: they are so obsessed by public affairs that they see the world as by moonlight, which shows the outlines of every object but not the details indicative of their nature." (Dame Rebecca, just, though seldom fair, also said: "the word *idiot* comes from a Greek root meaning private person. Idiocy is the female defect: intent on their private lives, women follow their fate through a darkness deep as that cast by malformed cells in the brain.")

Russia is suffering from a plethora of "the male defect:" lunatic theorizing about public affairs. "Private life," that "darkness" favored by West's women, Pushkin's "mousey scurrying," will, serve here to present some details indicative of Russia's nature. In Krasnodar.

Krasnodar: "beautiful gift," where we went, Diana and I and our two children, to direct a college language study program, is south. Tomatoes are available until December. It's near the Crimea and the Black Sea and, nevertheless, a contiguous part of the Russian Federation headed by Putin. It seems a dirty, ill-mannered, insect-ridden, 800,000 person provincial hole. Close up though, it is unusually, humanly warm. The *komandant* or manager of the dormitory where we lived, Natasha, met us with two pails of hot water when we arrived. The municipal hot water was turned off for the month of September, while the pipes were cleaned. Natasha thought we might want to wash up after fourteen hours in the air. She turned out to be one of our fates, a Red Goddess of our time in Krasnodar, and those two very welcome buckets of hot water were only the first of a succession of "beautiful gifts."

The job was administrative, not usually my department. The Rector of Kuban State University was an autocrat in the ancient Russian tradition. No one took action, publicly at least, without his "DA!" He, it turned out, had winkled a Fulbright out of the collapsing Soviet system and shortly decamped for Columbus, Ohio. Being an autocrat, he would, by definition and nature, not delegate authority. There were, at KGU, deans and vice-rectors, but they were absolutely decorative, and we needed, as it turned out:

1) A head teacher to coordinate the students' Russian studies;

2) Satisfactory organization of thirty days of field trips to Moscow, Pyatigorsk, Kiev;

3) Russian schools for our children;

4) A refrigerator, shelves, plates, light bulbs, window glass, and cheese; and

5) The liquidation of the discotheque forty feet from our window.

It seems that we spent four months *needing* in Krasnodar. The Rector, had he been present, could have solved these problems with a word, but he, like the Soviet system, had disappeared. (He had, before his secret and silent departure, thrown us a feast. In this respect, he was superior to the Soviet system.) His "DA!" and "NYET!" he took with him. So much, for now for the squalid details indicative of our reality's vacancies, the ineluctable fine print with which "idiot" women might concern themselves. Now for the pale, male, lunatic ideology of our situation, the big picture.

In seven years, from the inception of Gorbachev's *perestroyka* or revamping, the Soviet system, order and power, *poryadka* and *vlast*, dissolved. Yeltsin declared the Communist party illegal in Russia, which country he also made independent of the Soviet Union, in 1991. The framework that many men lived by, and extracted perquisites and prestige from was suddenly gone. Real winners, competitors, warriors, like our Rector who had, under Gorbachev, glumly supported *perestroyka* or reform of the party, now hastened to become democrats. Indeed, the word *democrat* is most often used, in Russian, to denote agile former party members or supporters. Followers, members of the *Komsomol*, young Communists-to-be, were left with a great vacuum where their faith once lived. Dissidents, oppositionists, of which there were always relatively few, were doubly orphaned. They were left without a clear enemy and with no old boys' network like that of the former party men. They had no one to help them into the coming market age. This led, among true believers, socialist or dissident, to cynicism, to alcoholism and, most strikingly, to inertia. At the university, more particularly, the absence of the Rector meant that there was no one to provide teachers, organize field trips, find us cheese and refrigerators. Lacking the autocrat, the machine languishes.

There are the fates, Pushkin's *parki*: the women in Krasnodar. (The Russian word for *person* is not *man* but *chelovyek*, a skull that lasts a lifetime. A *human being* then is not a *man* but rather a *mortal*.) The operative *mortals* in our lives, the savers of situations, turned out to be female. The Vice-rector, the Dean of Foreign Students, the Chairman of the Faculty of

Russian for Foreign Students, steamed fiercely but remained motionless. Lydia Stepanovna, the Rector's secretary, saw to it that the increasingly bitter complaints in my faxes to the head office in Chicago were translated and sent to the Rector in Columbus *before* they got to Chicago. This unheard of, but very effective, invasion of privacy led to the resolution of my teacher problem, the organization of a two-week Moscow-Leningrad field trip, an excursion to Kiev, even to the discovery of a refrigerator for the students and the silencing of the pestiferous discotheque. Olga, an English teacher, found a school for our children and sent her daughter and son, Anya and Andrey, to accompany, translate for, and be friends with our Sarah and David. Vera, a slapdash cleaning lady, made the drunken dormitory carpenter find shelf boards for our cabinets, glass for our windows, and even lent Diana a meat grinder to make pesto. The large, somewhat disorganized staff of concierges, linen ladies, and scrubbers advised marvelously on the variety and cheapness of foods in the various peasant markets and state stores, on quality haircuts, the preparation of mushrooms and when to avoid them (fourteen people died of polluted mushrooms in the Krasnodar hospitals) and where to find eggs. All of them taught us Russian. Vika, a research assistant in mathematics, provided a ten-course vegetarian feast from her herb-potato-greens-eggplant-onion-tomato-watermelon garden. (A single parent, Vika worked and harvested her garden, enduring an eighty-minute bus commute to get to it, before and/or after a day of mathematical research.) Raissa, secretary in the office for foreign students, locked her ten-year-old son in their apartment (he escaped out the window) to spend a full Saturday on our precious telephone trying to arrange hotel accommodations in Moscow for Diana and a sick student. Tatyana Vasilyevna, our head teacher, contributed five hours a week to tutor David and Sarah in Russian. Bird cherry, *kalina*, for Diana's sore throat, pasta, dishes, light bulbs, telephone repairs, books, tea and sympathy: the fates of Krasnodar provided all of these things, *defisit* items, not available on the market. Lydia, Olga, Vera, Vika, Natasha and Tatyana organized our survival, but these details need, again, to be added up. We turn once more from idiocy to lunacy, the male world.

The Dean of Foreign Students was a far more effective teacher than he was an administrator. In a lecture on the dissolution of socialism in Russia, he asserted that Marxism is a bourgeois ideology because its governing councils, *sovyety,* are made up of people who think of themselves as individuals first of all. The traditional Russian ruling body, the *mir,* that we might call a kinship group or village assembly or, now, a *network,* is not. He meant that Marx saw socialist order as a grouping of proletarians for mutual benefit while the *mir,* which in Russian tradition antedates individualistic consciousness, is a prior, even tribal grouping. Its members have seldom known the possibility of individual survival, nuclear success. The dean claimed that Marxism failed in Russia just because it pre-supposed individualism, gave party men the opportunity to seek individual economic advantage, as famously delineated by Djilas in *The New Class,* and thus short-circuited the *mir,* the small local community which experienced, survived or perished, as a group.

The *mir* is a much-discussed phenomenon in Russian history. Its centrality or irrelevance and even its existence are hotly debated. The concept of the *mir* appears in this place because it seems, to me, and it seemed to my students in Krasnodar, to be central to the way in which women, at least, survive now in Russia. Let, for want of a more academic source, John Le Carré's *Russia House* speak here:

She became Katya the provider. On Mondays there was a chance of fresh chickens and vegetables brought privately from the country over the weekend. Her friend Tanya had a cousin who functioned informally as a dealer for smallholders. Phone Tanya.

...As soon as she got to the office she would collect two tickets for the Philharmonic which the editor Barzin had promised her as amends for his drunken advances at the May Day party...

...At lunchtime after shopping she would trade two tickets with the porter Morozov, who had pledged her twenty-four bars of imported soap wrapped in decorative paper. With the fancy soap she would buy the bolt of green check cloth of pure wool that the manager of the clothing shop was keeping locked in his storeroom for her. Katya resolutely refused to wonder why. This afternoon... she would hand the cloth to Olga Stanislavsky, who, in return for favors to be negotiated, would make two cowboy shirts on the East German sewing machine she had recently traded for her ancient family Singer, one for each twin in time for their birthday. And there might even be enough cloth left over to squeeze them both a private check-up from the dentist. (Bantam, 1990, pp. 135-6.)

***

Natasha our dormitory *komandant*, Vera, the cleaning lady, Lydia, the Rector's secretary-- all of our women friends lived in *mirs*, self-sustaining worlds like that of Le Carré's Katya. (*Mir* can mean traditional community, world even *peace*. It is profitable to think about the relationships between these meanings.) In the fall of 1991, an average Russian wage was three hundred rubles a month. This was about half of what a person needed to survive so the women *networked*, to use the American barbarism, and again, like Le Carré's Katya, cared for Uncle Matvey who slept on the parlor couch, usually waking up with a hangover.

This is too black and white, idiotic or lunatic, too female and male altogether: not human, mortal enough. Our dormitory Natasha's husband, Sasha, a Red Army colonel in charge of the Military Science program at KGU, genuinely worked as a teacher, netted and brought home for drying or canning bushel baskets of walleyed pike, cooked, washed dishes, and restored order when fists or nailed boards flew in the dormitory. Olga's husband, Misha, a painter of glowing water-color landscapes, also fished for food, prepared the salad for guest dinners, and played regularly, barefoot and boisterous, with his children and ours. The Rector himself was, if anything, hyperactive. He ruled the university, had published two authoritative books on abstruse mathematical issues, kept up Moscow contacts with Communist old boys, served as a People's Deputy in the parliament, and fended for his own *mir,* which included Lydia his secretary, Natasha her daughter, a chauffeur, the gardening Vika who was his research assistant, a beekeeper, two vintners, as well as a wife, two children, and an aunt in New Jersey. The *mir* world, the exchange of information, goods, influence, and encouragement, that makes life bearable, *does* include men, but not usually. Usually, this nurturing community, *literally* nurturing, is kept up by women.

Rebecca West or, today, Ursula Le Guin, would say, I think, that men are interested in success, in power, in *winning* however defined. If they are not directly involved in these matters, they can at least follow politics, what we call *the big picture*, in masculine conversation or in the newspapers. Many are reduced to reading the sports pages. Mere daily survival is generally the concern of women. Deprived of the possibility or at least the depiction of success by the collapse of the socialist system, many men in Russia are, literally, at loose ends. Power and control, now lacking a central ideological authority, remain largely in the hands of the former party bosses, now become CEOs, and are reduced and localized. Former black marketeers, in the south the so-called Mafia, are laying the rough under-flooring for a developing market economy. Many men, neither former party bosses nor Mafia nor, like Sasha and Misha, androgynous enough to cooperate with women to ensure survival, despair and do nothing and drink.

These last, a great many Russian men of various backgrounds, one stumbled over in the dark or even at ten in the morning, easily sabotaged Gorbachev's early anti-alcohol initiative. These are the men of whom DuPlessis-Gray speaks in her *Soviet Women: Walking the Tightrope*. The proto-feminists whom she interviews in that work plan to bear a child and abandon the father. He is, they say, in any event drunk and shiftless, a mere liability. DuPlessis-Gray's informants no doubt exist in the more sophisticated Russian centers. In Krasnodar, with eight hundred thousand inhabitants but also eight hundred miles south of Moscow, women still seem to think otherwise.

A telling, sad, and favorite scene comes to mind. In the four o'clock rush hour, an early drunk has crashed with his head on the trolley tracks. A middle-aged woman in a kerchief carefully hauls him out of danger, retrieves his cigarettes, matches, and cap, replaces the former in the inside band of the latter, and sets the cap back on his still sleeping head. Then, she smiles and bustles off to the market across the street or perhaps home to prepare dinner. She was no relative of his. She was doing her duty, *Khrista radi*, for Christ's sake.

A further example: Tatyana Vasilyevna, head teacher, lecturer, and our children's tutor, had no particular reason to respect or defend men. It was, apparently, jealousy of her success with our language program, or just sheer cussedness, that moved her chairman, who taught American students badly, with no grasp of English, to fire her. When the president of our group of colleges urgently requested Tatyana's reinstatement, this chairman, the Dean Tarasov, and Comrade Blednick, reputed former KGB officer at the university, set upon her with verbal violence for endangering the American program with her complaints. She left the meeting where we had both been present tight-lipped and raging. Her chairman coolly informed me that she was like a daughter to him and it was time, at twenty-nine, for her to marry and have children. When Tatyana and I spoke of the matter later, she informed me, not being the "idiot" of West's stereotype, that Russian men suffer, mainly, from the last three generations of utterly female upbringing. Their natural male models, fathers and uncles and older brothers, were crippled or died in the world wars, the Russian Civil War, and the repeated purges. So raised, Russian men are simply, from Tatyana's point of view, spoiled, willful children. She herself unwittingly bolstered this generalization with her relative indulgence toward our son David in the tutorial sessions and in her assumption that his sister Sarah, older and more assiduous in learning the language, was only working as women are expected to do.

My students at Kuban State University came up with analogous data on the relations of the sexes in Russia. This group of American undergraduates, twenty women and seven men, interviewed Russians, mainly their peers, in preparation for a required paper on a sociological topic. Although the Russian divorce rate rivals ours, most of the Russian coeds interviewed looked forward to marriage and children, and also to a continuation of professional activity, usually in a teaching or other care-giving field.

Young Russian *men*, when interviewed, tended to see their only possible future in the nascent Russian free market and, often, were planning to escape to the mother of all free markets, the United States. Public service and the academic disciplines simply don't pay living wages at present, and positions in the applied sciences don't either. Activity in these areas, then, implies dependence upon the above-discussed *mir*, upon women's networking. Rather than more of this, many young men consider, for the first time in my experience of Russia, emigration.

If communal sharing, promoted largely by women, *is* central to survival in Russia now, why is it not publicly recognized? I don't know for sure, but again Ursula Le Guin, offers some hints. In a commencement address dealing with *our* male/female dichotomy, she illuminated problems endemic to both cultures:

Success is somebody else's failure. Success is the American Dream we can keep dreaming because most people, in most places, including thirty million of ourselves, live wide awake in the terrible reality of poverty. No, I do not wish you success. ...I want to talk about failure.

Women as women are largely excluded from, alien to, the self-declared male norms of this society...the so-called man's world of institutionalized competition, aggression, violence, authority and power. If we want to live as women, some separatism is forced upon us.

[O]ur terms...are not all rational, positive, competitive...In our society, women have lived, and have been despised for living, the whole side of life that includes and takes responsibility for helplessness, weakness, and illness, for the irrational and the irreparable, for all that is obscure, passive, uncontrolled, animal, unclean - the valley of the shadow, the deep, the depths of life. All that the warrior denies and refuses is left to us and the men who share it with us and therefore, like us, can't play doctor, only nurse, can't be warriors, only civilians, can't be chiefs, only Indians....

Ursula Le Guin, "A Left-Handed Commencement Address"

***

Le Guin's depiction of men's and women's worlds is, you see, in some ways analogous to the world of Krasnodar in 1991. One large difference is that the male institutions of competition and power, except for the communist old boy's network and the Mafia (sometimes one and the same) have largely broken down, and women's responsibility for helplessness is the one "institution" which seems to be supporting "the mousey scurrying of life" at all. Those men who are most active are continuing a kind of clandestine party activity, while most men doze or drink in the absence of authority and of the excitement of the game of authority. The largely women's *mir*, the communal sharing and laboring which nourish everyday life, can hardly be celebrated because it has necessarily replaced and usurped traditional male prerogatives. Competition, for the moment, until the promised development of the free market, is the province of the Mafia, a rather secretive minority. Mutual aid, on a self-produced shoestring of gardening and knitting and standing in line, seems, nevertheless, much more central just now. "Idiocy" has put "lunacy" in the shade.

Susan Richards's fine *Epics of Everyday Life* provides, here, a fitting epilogue:

I had gone to Russia to understand a strange culture. I came back experiencing my own as if for the first time. I was more alarmed than impressed. Abundance seemed in so many ways harder to cope with than scarcity. Surrounded by a superfluity of trivial choices, it was hard to keep one's bearings. How would my Soviet friends survive in this world of pleasant surfaces and hard underlying realities? I found myself fearing lest contact with the West should undermine the qualities in them that I had come to appreciate the most.

The other side of the same question also kept returning to me. How might our culture be affected by contact with this other world? Having experienced the generosity of people who had nothing, I had arrived back thinking how little our prosperous society knew about giving. What chance was there that we would have the humility to learn from these people who lived in the wreckage of a dream that had failed?

CHAPTER IX

Queuing Up: The West in Krasnodar, 1991

"He is already too much a French." Lydia Stepanovna, the rector's secretary, said this with the slight twinkle that meant, I had learned, that here she couldn't help. She had decided that I would have to bear with this man, with his habits, with my fate, *sudba*. Of Slavic extraction myself, I was half inclined to agree. However, my wife Diana's maiden name is Kessler. The name is German, and it implies order and competence, which are, with some lovely exceptions, the air she breathes. What was to be done? "Nothing-*nichevo*-it doesn't matter," said Russia around me. Diane said otherwise.

Lydia Stepanovna became my right hand when I tried to manage the Russian language program for American students at Kuban State University. Though he presided over an array of deans, the Rector, like any autocrat when pressed, left government to an intimate rather than a system. Lydia Stepanovna *was* Rector in the Rector's absence. (When we toured Moscow, she spent two weeks at her *dacha* and took the university safe with her!) I have earlier attested to her support in the matter of a refrigerator, teachers, cheese, and light bulbs. Lydia Stepanovna was, as we used to say, *key*.

What about this "too much a French?" He was our suite-mate, who arrived in the middle of the 1991 fall semester to enrich our lives and make us a part of *France d'outre mer*. Diana and I, with our children Sarah and David, lived in a dormitory for foreign students. It was surrounded by mud, weeds, broken glass and, at night, *The Grateful Dead*. Our "suite," a narrow passage parallel to the main corridor of the first floor as a "pocket" is to the large intestine in colitis, was made up of our bedroom, the children's bedroom, a living-dining cubicle, and the Frenchman's room. A narrow passageway, connected at each end with the main corridor, ran between these four rooms and a lineup of toilet, sink, and shower (short rubber hose and hole in the floor.) In his all-too-Frenchness, our suite-mate was obstructing both the main corridor and this smaller passage with a succession, no, a queue, of Russian coeds and non-coeds. These visitors walked noisily on spiked heels, smoked the odorous *makhorka* for lack of *Gitanes*, and yowled like lynxes while "visiting." Their passion drowned out the strains of Massenet and even the baroque drum rolls of Rameau on our neighbor's tape player. Finally, they stuffed our pitiful straw wastebaskets with Soviet champagne bottles, wilted roses, and condoms; the remains of their house gift offerings at this furthest outpost of the *Legion étrangère*. It was the smoke, noise, and mess that most affected Diana. (*I* was afflicted with uncomprehending jealousy.) We were moved, then, to rid ourselves of this Frenchman, but translated faxes or not, Lydia Stepanovna could not help this time.

Why not? Well, even in the blossoming of the Soviet Union, space was hard to come by. Russians inquiring about our Wisconsin quarters asked in terms of "square meters of living space," not of whole rooms. When the Union melted like old ice in this autumn of 1991, space became even more precious. Meat, books, gasoline, living space, everything but bread, vodka, and sour cream, indeed, began to ebb more rapidly, as if the Soviet economy, like a leaking hydroelectric dam that Brezhnev ignored and Gorbachev tried to shore up, were swept away by utter bankruptcy. Power, future, and possibility seemed to float off together. Now, there was measurably, rapidly, less of everything. There was really no other place for the Frenchman to live.

In all honesty, our thirty students were utterly unfazed by this Russian shambles. Buoyed by youth, idealists all, they felt guilt at our relative affluence, and loved Russia for her holy poverty. My family's problem was, to *their* glorious spirit, no problem, but rather a joke. We, though, weren't students any longer, dammit.

We had, indeed, tried to *resolve* this horrendous difficulty in advance. Three rooms were hard enough to keep clean with the two-foot broom made of reeds from the Sea of Azov. This short implement was unable even to shift the black water bugs and gray cottonwood fluff (or was it asbestos?) that terminally littered the tatty red carpets. The Russian school regime of stressed-out, screeching teachers, the dark closet or a twisted ear as normal punishment, and a minimal knowledge of Russian, drove Sarah and David to a pitch of sibling rivalry unrecorded since Genesis. It was dangerous to make them share a room. Our laundry, lacking a Maytag, or even hot water, the city's cleaning of the hot water pipes having stretched through October, hung constantly in the upper reaches of all three rooms. We needed more space. The Frenchman's room beckoned as seductively as ever Bluebeard's pantry. At Diana's entreaty, threat, really, I laid siege to the Dean of Foreign Students for a full month before the Frenchman arrived.

Igor Ignatich, the Dean, said, variously: 1) that the Frenchman had not been rehired, 2) that he was coming to retrieve his belongings but not to stay, 3) that he would certainly be living here for the semester, 4) that he ought to arrive at the end of September, and 5) that there was no Frenchman. Some of this misinformation must be traced to my insufficient Russian, some to the Dean's Cossack dialect. However, most of my uncertainty was due to that ubiquitous and utterly necessary indifference to fact that alone makes life in *Rus* possible. The Dean went on: 1) we could have the extra room, 2) we would certainly never be granted that much living space, and 3) that there was no room, just the nasty courtyard beyond that beckoning door.

From a Russian perspective, of course, our request was inordinate. No one except the Rector had "a room of one's own." (And still, Akhmatova and Tsvetayeva, like Jane Austen, had written magnificently.) The best that we could expect, we were told, was that the Frenchman would not arrive. Russian honor demanded that his possessions remain inviolate, locked in that room but for all practical purposes, excepting the occupation of that room, we had the unheard of luxury of a whole suite for just our family. In Russian terms, this was an impossible and, probably, immoral expanse.

Feckless lunatic that I am, I felt the force of this argument even after the Frenchman arrived. Diana did not. She fried toasted cheese because a flour sauce she prepared with macaroni emitted both larvae and winged scions of larvae. She calmed me when I woke in the morning shouting an expletive that rhymes with "Yuck!" and fell asleep muttering "Yech!." She stroked the children through a Russian middle school where they knew little Russian, and queued where there was no food but black bread and sour cream. For Diana, I say, more space meant the vague possibility of a human life. I persisted in my attempt to move the Dean on the subject of the now all too present Frenchman, but I failed.

Tout comprendre c'est tout pardonner. I chose this cowardly route. The Frenchman was at once a foreign phenomenon and a comment on Russian life. If I could reach understanding, I might be able to bring Diana to forgiveness, of me, or, at the least, of my failure to disappear the Frenchman. Well, what was he, anyway? He looked like an under clerk at a bank, a small town mayor, the embodiment of *bourgeois.* He was slightly balding, had mushily indeterminate features, dressed in fuzzy, dusty grays, walked hesitantly, indeed, even tried to be friends, as a happy puppy might. His name was certainly not Raoul but the less suggestive Jean. He was decidedly lower-middle, like me. Why was there this constant lineup of bleached-blonde or henna-red, spike-heeled, green-eye-shaded, "Moscow Nights" exuding, *makhorka*-smoking, gift-bearing Slavic lovelies at his door, feet, disposal? This, when his mien, anything but Casanova-like, certainly not of the Sade school, vaguely bewildered, suggested not *machismo*, but the desire to flee? Indeed, the Dean reported that he was seeking an apartment away from the university, somewhere in the town.

In Russian parlance, a normal, regular, ordinary is *zlobodnyevny.* This is a biblical word, an adjective made of the saying: "Sufficient unto the day is the evil thereof." Throughout Russian history this word has suggested the *best* of possibilities. Thus, in a common Russian toast, a genuinely beautiful, happy day is apostrophized thus: "May this be the worst day you ever live." Life in Russia was, is, and can be expected to continue, hard far beyond American middle class comprehension. I speak not of the chance visitations of AIDS, cancer, or the occasional IRS audit. I'm referring to the evils of every day, soaplessness for instance, or a week-long search for eggs.

In the present economic shambles, as I've said earlier, ambitious Russian men who formerly placed their bets on party advancement, now put their money on the indigenous Mafia. The unambitious find a bottle and may be found happily boozing in a mud puddle on a rainy Sunday noon. Women, on the other hand, who traditionally carry the can or, more usually, the woven string shopping bag called an *avoska*, "perhaps," have bet on networking, gardening and standing in line for scarce commodities. "Scarce" means commodities that they can't raise in their *dacha* gardens: zippers, say, or a bottle of Armenian cognac for the man that they support, almost literally, on their shoulders. This kind of waiting, which seems to have been going on for the full thousand years of Russian Orthodoxy, has taught Russian women to wait and hope. Hell, it taught my son, David, these useful virtues, and although this account may seem a detour, it occurs to me that an apparent aside is just the route to an understanding of the Frenchman's magnetism, and of those women waiting inside and outside of our suite.

Life went on outside our beleaguered fortress, our smoke-filled suite. For lack of garbage disposals, for lack of newspaper or wrapping, there was a regular rain of potato peels and tomato fragments in the courtyard that lit our first-floor windows. Saturday nights the ex- and implosions of vodka and champagne bottles and of the glass from less innervating liquids made the evening "awesome" as even our nine-year-old son learned to say. However, those vessels which did not break on impact became the foundation of David's contribution to the barely burgeoning "free market" in this former Soviet Union. He began to gather bottles and return them for the deposits to the "collection point."

David had the right slipperiness for his market venture. He not only gleaned the courtyard, he cruised the American students' rooms accepted, then unnoticed. He passed through the common kitchens of the dormitory like a small shadow. He cleared the yard of unsmashed glass daily, mornings, when the hail of trash was thinner, and I suspect him of frequenting student parties late in the evening and even of emptying bottles when the liquid levels dropped too slowly to suit him. (I never accused him of this so he never had to deny it.) When the passage within our suite was almost terminally obstructed by the detritus of the offerings to the Frenchman *and* David's gleanings, it was time to load a bushel-size string bag with, perhaps, fifty half-liter bottles. Then, since he could not afford to hire one of the bony horses still visible on the fringes of dissolving collective farms not far from the university, he loaded me up with a humungous "perhapska" for the journey to the collection point: *sobiratyelny punkt.*

It was at this stage of his endeavors that David and I began to imbibe the patience and hope that queuing has taught Russian women. The collection points opened, closed, and shifted location with a fine irregularity. When

David tracked down an open *punkt,* it was quite often closed by the time he got me there with a load of bottles. Sometimes, instead of a queue of women laden with glass, there would be a queue of men, for a few of the "bottle ladies" practiced ancillary trades behind the wooden vodka cases. In that situation, the wait in line might be very long: two hours, say. However, if David were alone carrying a David-sized *avoska,* the bottle lady might well interrupt her more lucrative business, wave the men away like flies, and buy David's bottles for double the going rate. Such is the power of a small boy over a female Russian heart. Anyway, it often occurred that David, or David and I, would *not* go home happy. Our queuing on those days led to nothing at all in the form of deposit rubles. On the days when the *punkt* was open, and in funds, we danced all the way home.

During these journeys along the muddy paths that led to our university, head down because fully loaded with the bushel *avoska,* or because of economic disappointment, I began to notice elaborate patterns of tiny, hoof-shaped depressions incised in the trails. These patterns disappeared in dry weather, but it wasn't often dry. With inclement times they multiplied. Finally, I realized that these diminutive pony tracks were left by spike-heeled shoes. Since a goodly number of such impressions came together; from all directions, at the entrance to our dormitory, I knew that I had come upon the main routes of pilgrimage to Paris. Once more, I collided with the mystery of the Frenchman's spell.

In this account of life in Krasnodar, I have been so involved in the world of physical fact, so driven by the search for black bread, eggs, living space, and bottles, that I had almost forgotten that my trade is Russian literature, a joy, but an activity that sometimes makes for spiritual pretension. Three years after we returned from southern Russia, I found, I think, a part of the explanation of the Russian successes of French culture. This explanation is also involved with David's bottle fortune, which, by the way, was dissipated largely on ice cream, though not, I guess, on the dirty kind that a disillusioned Anna Karenina likened to life.

It happened that I read a work by Mikhail Kuraev. The work is called "Captain Dikshtein," appears in Margareta O. Thompson's translation of Kuraev's *Night Patrol and Other Stories*, published by Duke University Press in 1994. A central passage in this work deals with the bottle trade:

There was hardly anyone in the line who wasn't experiencing the warm joy of success....The right to return empty glass containers and receive either nine or and twelve kopecks seems like a trifling one, but if you deprive someone of this right or make it complicated for him to use it, then at once a slight taste of bitterness and vexation is added to the joyful savoring of life. It is just that man is constructed in the very worst possible way: the happiness he gets when he manages to return his bottles easily is, like many kinds of happiness - transitory. It doesn't leave an impression and doesn't lighten up even a single hour of his life; but mundane difficulties and burdens are capable of poisoning the entire day. And this continual blind game with fate engenders excitement in some, in others an enterprising effort worthy of admiration, and in still others a dull resignation and an unvoiced, unspoken resentment.

(pp. 11-12)

***

It was just this joy at success in the "continual blind game with fate" that the Russian coeds, and not-coeds, were experiencing. The Frenchman was not "too much a French" as Lydia Stepanovna thought. I think that he embodied, for these women, European romance, escape from the "bitterness and vexation." During the tour of Moscow and St. Petersburg with our students in 1991, we found the queues for McDonald's and Pizza Hut to be block-long, but the lines before small Lancôme banners stretched, literally, for a kilometer. Here were those same Russian women, smoking, tight-skirted, in spike heels, feeding their dreams. What could we, who were awake, possibly say to these Francophiles?

CHAPTER XI

Krasnodar Once More: 1997

"Of course," Natasha said, "he loved me more than I loved him."

"Of course," I blurted, "why 'of course'?"

"Because he gave up more: a family, a general's rank, which no divorced man could expect to attain in the Red Army, and valuable connections."

He gave up more, he loved more, a definition. Cripes, ten visits to Russia, three years spent here out of the last thirty, and I'm still so ignorant of the place.

I was back teaching, well, doing an abominable job of administrating, in Krasnodar. My friend Alexander (Sasha) died at fifty-three of a stroke while I was away. I was talking to his widow Natasha, one of the Red Goddesses who made life possible here for my family and me in 1991, as the Soviet Union fell apart. Russia, as opposed to the Union, was still here. "Of course."

This place. Mud, not sidewalks, mostly. The manhole covers have returned, but they must not be walked upon. They regularly tip and throw pedestrians into sewage or, sometimes, boiling sewage. (The year before a little girl died, in the hospital, of burns so received.) The traffic, and people go without cheese to buy gasoline, is made up of inexperienced drivers piloting Russian-made Fiats (Ladas) and they never dreamed of anti-pollution devices. It follows that there is little air. Elevators halt more regularly between floors than is the case in the West, but there are proportionately fewer of them. Zebra stripes, directional signals, and protective handrails, are almost nonexistent. *You* look out. Our "jungle out there" is, relatively, a joke, and in the midst of this "He gave up more."

Natasha, I realize, is a good example of the Russia I have loved for fifty-five years. Moscow, now becoming Los Angeles on the Moskva River, is not. Of course, Natashas can be found there, too. Life doesn't change nearly as quickly as we imagine. The *new Russians,* a term coined by the Natashas for those who have utterly embraced consumerism and abandoned human solidarity, are, like these Natashas themselves, not that new either. Stalin gave up early on the principal of equal pay. I have met "operators" here since 1961, *tolkachi* who bartered mercury for steel, workers for contracts, who were crucial in helping their factories almost meet Soviet norms, and who were paid in cars and percentages. The famous Russian Mafia, too, used to work for the Party, man the KGB, and inhabit the widespread "criminal" underground, whatever that can mean in an essentially lawless society. No, I'm not on about changes in Russia nearly as much as about Russia *per se.* Or so I fondly imagine. Again, I feel pretty ignorant.

On the other hand, there were striking material changes. Moscow, a major outpost of the free market, bends under its load of McDonald's and Pizza Huts. Even worse, to my temperament, was the shiny new Christ the Savior Cathedral built to replace the one Stalin blew up. Khruschev filled the space with an all-weather outdoor swimming pool. (It was said, in 1961, that the former monks lurked in the steam clouds in winter to drown careless blasphemers.) This church, like the removal of monuments to Lenin and Dzerzhinsky, suggested that the Revolution didn't happen, that we've always been free marketeers together, that Orthodox bishops have always blessed new Mercedes automobiles. Russia has, since my last visit in 1991, surpassed the United States in civilian firearms deaths. It was the first country in the world to do so. In her novel *Moo*, one of Jane Smiley's characters opines that Americans "are the only people in the world who are surprised when people are people." She means, when people are predators. I am surprised when they are not. That's why I began this 1997 Krasnodar journal with Natasha.

That evening, then, I was invited to dinner by an old friend, Natasha, my colonel's widow. I carried cold champagne and an odd number of red roses, because an even number of flowers portends bad luck in Russia. I walked the dirt sidewalks of back alleys, bordered just then by raggedy black-eyed susans and last primroses. In tiny courts behind the main street's buildings were benches with couples and *babas* of all ages keeping tabs on running, shouting children. Away from the noisome traffic I found Friday night peace.

Two buddies were carrying a lawn chair and jointed fishing poles. A third, in a car, pulled over to ask if they'd sell their expected fish. They said that they had already, in expectation, drunk up, *propili,* the expected rubles from the expected fish. Girls much more fashionably slender than I remembered, some on last year's clunky English heels, strolled, arm in arm: also fishing. It was Friday night indeed.

Natasha, the *komandant* of Dormitory #4, where we had lived six years ago, opened her door decked out in a lacy, angora sweater and checked skirt, low-heeled matron's shoes. (Russians wear *tapochki*, soft carpet slippers, at home, but not for parties.) I produced the bubbly and Hershey waffle cookies for five-year-old Matvey. (Sasha, the colonel, was named Alexander Matveyevich. His long-desired son is Matvey Alexandrovich.) Matvey was quick and clever, *shustrij*, like a red squirrel, usually muddy, best buds with a troop of Vietnamese kids whose parents study agriculture here. He smiled, but was reserved with me, the strange "uncle," *dyadya*. He trotted off with some of his chocolate spoils.

Natasha was hostess, mom, and always *komandant*, so she accepted the champagne warmly but suggested, this once, cognac with dinner, actually a very good Greek brandy, because, I guess, she saw it as even more festive than champagne. She warned Matvey, a close casting of the gone but-also-here Colonel Sasha, about mud and resolved two dormitory disputes while perfecting dinner in the common kitchen down the hall. She is large, but not fat, oval-faced like a Modigliani, both deliberate and quick, uses "kh" instead of "g": "*khovorit,*" a sound that her Cossack ancestors brought here when Catherine gave them Ekaterinodar, now Krasnodar but soon to revert again. Sasha, the colonel, had been a *moskvich*, "but not uppity, like most of those people from the center."

Dinner began with smoked sturgeon and pearly black caviar on tiny ovals of French bread with a curl of yellow butter at one corner. If this shouldn't be enough of snacks, *zakuski*, there was also black bread, real Edam and Hungarian salami. Then came a fine beef goulash with yellow, real European potatoes. Dessert was a fresh-made apricot pie. Oof, Russian dinners are no joke.

I stood to toast Sasha, there's a photograph of him in full uniform on the wall, as I had never seen or imagined him, clinked glasses, but then Natasha stopped me. "This first one to our reunion, to life and the future. And, when *we* drink to the dead, we don't touch glasses." They are clearly beyond luck. "To us, then!" She drank, unhurried, but to the bottom. I did the same. Just this first one. Natasha's next toast was: "May the earth lie upon him like thistledown." (Cripes, is everything a rite? Yes, a good, a real one. One also makes spitting sounds over the left shoulder for luck, after praise, and one doesn't *ever* shake hands, pass, or accept things across a threshold. In Russia, these are no jokes, though my ignorance has been regularly forgiven.)

Food and talk in this room with hanging, good oriental rugs, is warm and cozy, but by no means well-to-do; everything there was earned slowly. Talk, my God. Sasha's sudden stroke. Yeltsin's by-pass that could have saved him. Average age, at death, of Russian men, is now 56. Sasha was 58 when he died in 1995, and that was then the statistical death age. In Soviet times, it was said to be 70 for men and 75 for women. Deaths in Chechnya, now in Abkhasia, as the Russian army is wasted, affect the statistics, but anomie, vodka and bad cigarettes do, too.

After the formal military funeral, promises of help came to nothing. She finished building their house by herself. One Ossetian buddy did help but now he's stationed in Abkhasia with the Russian peacekeepers who are shot on sight by both warring sides, Georgian and Abkhasian. As Natasha is on duty most days, at all hours and Matvey is, "thanks God," (her only English) a serious handful, she has breath to miss Sasha only morning and evening. He is there, then, and always, in Matvey, of course. They had eleven years together. This is where she speaks of Sasha's superiority in love. "He gave up wife, daughter, important friends, military perks of car, apartment, travel (Sasha had been stationed in Germany, Cuba, Mongolia, and finally Afghanistan over a long career). Then there was the certainty of a future general's rank, the pleasures, hardly, to Sasha, of received obedience and commanded respect. Natasha gave up less (had less to give) so she considered herself to have loved less. In that sense, her "of course." Only in that. Loving is giving. Why do I seek wisdom in academia?

Because divorce was frowned upon for army officers, Sasha was removed from the active army and given the State University Military Science Department to chair, and that was only because he had friends in high places. These connections were seriously strained earlier when Sasha, outraged by a dangerous grenade throwing exercise in which a recruit was killed, refused to engage in a cover-up. "He was a man!" However, *machismo* did have its difficulties. At the birth of a child, a ritual called "washing the baby" is sometimes practiced, a bit like handing out cigars. Though Sasha was unusually abstemious, he had, as a popular officer, many buddies, and he had long desired a son. While Natasha was still in the maternity ward with Matvey, Sasha "washed the baby" among friends, consuming with them, over several days, a case of vodka and another of Armenian cognac. On her return home, Natasha vetoed a second case of cognac. Even ritual has its limits.

She, alone except for Matvey, visits his grave on all great church holidays and on the monthly anniversary of his death, July 21, 1995. She weeps then, *otvodit serdtse*, "empties her heart," and is replenished by Sasha's thereness. Natasha believes that such weeping is the strength of women. Men, who cannot weep so, die, of course, younger. Again, women must live, for who otherwise would raise the children?

Ech! Many other things. She remembered my former assistant here, an economics professor, who had little spoken Russian though he understood well. He is a warm presence: a *zolotoy chelovyek* , a golden man. He's also something of a tease: "He's attractive because he's a bachelor (a *kholostoy*, an empty cartridge hull, a blank, needing to be filled.) Every co-ed wanted to take him home, as did half the Russian feminine population. Elena, dark, opulent, like marzipan, gifted, quick, didn't get him "because she's no trapper."

Then, Natasha, Orthodox, straight-arrow, nevertheless fills me in on new expressions:

Keif: one's criminal delight. Keifnut': to indulge it.

tasovatsya: to indulge one's criminal delight in company, at a non-straight gathering. This word's first meaning is "to shuffle the cards."

***

Then, back to Sasha. When Matvey was born, Natasha wanted to baptize him. Sasha had never been a believer. Baptism is impossible if both parents have not been baptized. "I came home and said "Well?" "*Nu?*"" Sasha was baptized on the same day as Matvey.

Matvey stroked Sasha's face in the coffin, as he lay in military state: epaulets, medals (for real bravery) stripes, boots (*sapogakh*), and all. *"Eto moy Papa."* Damn it to Hell!

Natasha, anticommunist, no, simply, as a believer unable to belong to *both* churches, hates the class, money divisions that now divide Russia, pities and helps the poor, as many as she can. Before, "everyone had a crust of bread, warm clothing," but not now. She longs for unity, for general, mutual love and forbearance.

"We have become so beastly to each other in the market. We disregard the queue, grab, live, as we did not under Socialism, for *rags.*" By "rags" Natasha refers to all conspicuous consumption: "Who needs three coats? We have forgotten to be a people, a community." Yes, here that old shibboleth of the Slavophile, the *mir*, the extended peasant community, appears. I, a "golden ager" in Wisconsin, remember a village where people were by no means *better*, but lived with the knowledge that they needed each other's help, and although modulating this need with large doses of sulfurous gossip, acted accordingly. Now, we need only, but very much, affordable health insurance, which disappeared in Russia, too, and guaranteed retirement, because we have neither neighbors nor kin in the former sense, and have become free, nuclear individuals: predators and prey.

Here is one more word: *krutoy:* abrupt, the New Russian. People like my student Jeremy who almost got me shot outside nasty Moscow. Matvey, kids in general, use the word to mean "dashing, painfully good," as in "Why can't we have a *krutoy* car like Uncle Ibrahim?" (the Ossetian officer now in Abkhasia.) Just as "wicked" was used by New England kids, bad becomes good: very, very desirable. Ying-yang. (Natasha tells a joke about uncles in Georgia: all the many uncles of the joke's protagonist are Georgians except one, who is a *"new Russian."*)

When I finally left, there was a bottle of the Greek brandy and a pile of Kuban peaches in my briefcase. ("Kuban" is the name of this area and its river.) Natasha simply wouldn't grasp my stupid "no's." I was also invited to Sasha's birthday feast at the cemetery on September 21. I walked home grieving, but filled, informed, "as light as thistledown."

The next day, Irina Alexandrovna, one of the American group's teachers, led a city tour. The day was sunny, warm, an early Indian summer, called "granny's summer" here. The bus was old, hot and cramped. Twenty-three of us shared eighteen seats. Irina was elected to introduce us to the geography, history, and present life of Krasnodar. Tatyana, the head teacher, then asked me to go along as translator, but the teachers spent the morning preparing the kids with the necessary vocabulary, and Irina's slow, clear delivery did the rest. I didn't need to translate much.

Catherine the Great *gave* this land (but whose was it?) to the Zaporozhe Cossacks about the time of the American Revolution. (Their robbing and raiding ways were a nuisance on the Dnieper river, in the Ukraine.) A wooden fort was built first. Catherine proved right in her belief that the Cossacks could take this forest and steppe land and make it theirs, and so, of course, hers. Later, once the native Muslim Adigey were pushed to the left (south) bank of the Kuban, where they still live, Krasnodar (at that time Ekaterinodar for "Catherine's Gift") became a city open to all, surrounded by rich farms, a trading center, a melting pot of Greeks, Armenians, Jews, Poles, and other ethnic groups.

Ornate brick buildings from Catherine's time and later, Soviet cement horrors, and the new brick condominiums or private mansions of the New Russians, vary the cityscape. We lurched along the main street, here *Krasnaya* because freed by the Red *(Krasnaya)* Army in 1943, until we reached Gorky Park and a monument to the eight thousand military dead of that victory. A twenty-foot cement tommy-gunner backed by riflemen stands above the names of the regiments involved. The Catherinian language of "fusiliers," and "dragoons" was still used in naming these units.

Irina's story was well rehearsed, simplified for us, clearly told, at throat-shaking volume near busy Krasnaya Street. It was mostly about "The Great Fatherland War," to distinguish it from the war with Napoleon, which is "The Fatherland War." The students, it seemed to me, listened bemused to this ancient history, which was, incredibly enough, played out live when I was ten.

Suddenly, *vdrug*, a thin, urgent *baba* in black, her boney face wrapped in a blue kerchief, was muttering to Tyler, a kindly, shy student at one edge of our crowd. As Irina tried to lead the group, addressed as *druzya moi* - "my friends" - to another monument in Gorky Park, I, always playing rearguard, moved to find out what the *baba* wanted with Tyler, who looked perplexed. Russian, but lately from Baku, Azerbaizhan, she said she fought here during the liberation.

Skinny, frail, sharp as a dagger, she denounced this monument to the heroic dead, wished impossibly, unspeakably, that Hitler had *won*, since the living, the survivors like herself and her invalid husband, could not live on the hundred dollars a month that their two pensions bring. As their daughter was studying medicine here on a tiny grant, they chipped together to survive, barely, in a single dormitory room. She showed me her identity card: the photo of a round, rosy Russian matron that she, this skeleton, used to be. "What about the living? Gorbachev, Yeltsin betrayed us, betrayed our victory over Fascism! That Hitler, God save me, *should* have won." She was trying to set Irina's history in present perspective. *I* said that I would try to write, to tell her story as best I could. She blessed me, wished my pen the lightness, quickness of down, *pukh*, that is, of a feather, which is here as in English, also the word for a pen.

In the tiny, tinny bus I told Irina about this woman, and released a flood: "True, all true, and the pity that such words can be rightly said of our victory. Now *having* for the few takes the place of the giving, sharing, the feeling of each having enough. We are Orthodox in feeling, not protestant 'achievers,' and though I belong to no church, I know that in poor Russia, cut off, always, from Europe and Asia, one pair of shoes, not five, and one loaf, is enough. That's Orthodoxy! How can I stand to look at these brick condominia, and these Mercedes cars? We are losing what is most essential to us: our hearts." Irina echoed the colonel's widow. I could only agree.

In the course of her tour, Irina referred, negatively, to the present fashion of changing back to pre-revolutionary names, to the destruction of Soviet monuments. She felt that it was an attempt to adulterate history not unlike the earlier attempts of the Communists. Then she pointed out a bronze bust of Felix Dzerzhinsky, " first head of the Cheka." (The Cheka was the ancestor of the KGB, the secret police. An early action of the newly freed Russians, in 1990, was the destruction of the huge statue of Dzerzhinsky that stood in the square before the Lubyanka, KGB headquarters in Moscow, "that sad building," as Vitaly's Moscow secretary referred to it.)

"Surely, Dzerzhinsky's bust could go, Irina Viktorovna!"

"I don't think so. He should remain, if only as a warning. There was more to him than the Cheka. Dzerzhinsky set up schools for orphaned children, *bezprizorniki*, during the Revolution and the Civil War. Those schools saved thousands of lives. Even *he* was a good man, in part." Again she explained that the Bolsheviks also renamed and destroyed monuments and, in doing so, did deadly violence to the historical truth.

Our last stop was a soccer field where "the Fascists" (they are seldom referred to as Germans,) set up closed trucks in which they gassed old people and children left in Krasnodar, when the able-bodied retreated. The Russians called these vehicles "soul-killers," *dushegubtsi,* because the victims died without last rites.

"One man, excuse me," she begged "wet his shirt with his own urine, breathed through it, played dead, crawled out of the common grave and, after the war, gave testimony at the war crimes trials. He saw a few of the butchers hung." My students and I, and this was to recur often, found nothing quite adequate to respond to this. There was nothing in our experience *like* this. Still, I never heard any particular hatred of present-day Germans, certainly not of German visitors or tourists, from Russians.

Indeed, Irina's strictures were reserved mostly for contemporary Russians. As we started back to the university after our tour, Irina pointed out a street in the northern part of town where one man with a machine gun held up the attacking Fascists from the ruins of a bombed out house. When he finally surrendered, the German soldiers saluted him. The point of this story, for Irina, was that "this man died *alone* a few years ago. His body was found accidently by repairmen. To die *alone* after such heroism." Her eyes added, sadly: "Yes, we Russians have come even to this." I remembered the old woman who shouted "Gorbachev, Yeltsin betrayed us. Hitler should have *won.*"

A week or so later, a stranger shouted "Yatzeck," as I met the students before the main entrance of Kuban State University, our regular nine AM date. (Uncomfortable with titles, I've asked them to call me Yatzeck. This has, apparently, spread.) The man, beefy, good stainless steel smile, wanted me to translate the messages appearing on the built-in computer screen of his handsome, steel-gray BMW. Because the messages were in German and only mildly technical, I could help. He, naturally, had thought them to be in English and, anyway, aren't all *nemtsy* alike? The messages: "replace brake linings," "add cold water to radiator," "top up windshield cleaner." The beast spoke, German even! What an advance on asphyxiation trucks! What Natasha would call "rags."

My conversations with Russians in Krasnodar were occasional and unofficial, of course. I didn't really recognize public utterance as conversation. Though I've made my living as a lecturer, or because I have, I'm convinced that the life-revealing *private* exchange of experience is alone fruitful. Now, since the collapse of Soviet power, Russians love to talk. How lucky I felt to be able to understand!

It was in just such an accidental situation that I met the bank guard, Andrey. On my way home, I found Tadzhik dried apricots, amber raisins, and brown walnuts at the East market. I dumped the lot in a plastic bag carried "just in case," *avos*. I shook up my trail mix and realized that my rubles were running short. I'd have to go to the bank.

The "bank" was a small room behind a locked, steel, double door. One stood until one's turn came to sit on a long wooden bench. At extended intervals, the guard unlocked the half door, let a patron out, and beckoned to the next. People held each other's places. One might wait two hours to find that the rubles or dollars had just run out. Then, with the proper attitude oiling proper negotiations, one might return later and go to the head of the line.

Inside the steel door, there was just room for the guard, one patron, and a barred window. Having handed over one's passport, one might or might not change travelers' checks or dollars for rubles or rubles for dollars. As I waited for my rubles, the guard and I discussed the fine fall weather.

As it happened, the next noon I saw the guard at the cafe "Under the Linden Trees." In this cafe, the trees grow through the roof and are regularly sprinkled by the half-dozen dogs that frequent the place. In this casual atmosphere, the guard motioned me over.

Andrey was twenty-eight. He had been married, but decided present-day Russia was no place to raise children. She left him. Over a beer, two eggs and bread, $2.25, he told many stories:

Of the war: His uncle was killed while hopelessly attempting to cover a retreat before tanks with a light machine gun. Andrey noted that only humans make war, while animals of the same species fight to the death only when overcrowded. I asked him about the prevalence of hazing and sadistic punishment of recruits by non-commissioned officers in the Russian army. This had been a serious problem when I was here six years ago. Andrey laughed. "Too many sergeants were shot from behind during the war in Chechnya," he said. "Now, they mind their manners." He had served his required army time.

Andrey believed that Stalin was a psychopath, but he revered Lenin. Why are psychopaths rulers? Most gifted men are psychopaths, like Dostoevsky. Tolstoy was normal but nasty. He employed his natural son as a coachman.

When I asked about Cossack nationalists here in the Kuban, he said they were largely phonies, only interested in drinking "traditionally." Still, the old ways were best. "Our women smoke. Some even drink, now. The only real Russian women live in *stanitsy*, Cossack villages."

Remarks in passing: Eduard Limonov, Edik, is a writer who uses racy, contemporary speech. Though he has become "abnormal," a homosexual, he remains Andrey's favorite writer. (Edik distinguished himself more recently by joining the Serbian forces and becoming one of the sharpshooters who killed pedestrians in Sarajevo.)

Andrey's mother silenced him, when as a school child, he spoke of the need for Brezhnev to die. "Now we can at least talk." He goes on to assert that Pavlik Morozov (a Soviet icon) was no hero. His folks did well to kill him for reporting their conversations to the KGB. Here I repeated a local street madman's question: "Where is the street named after Pavlik Morozov's granddaughter?" Though my friend, Tanya, figured out that such a street couldn't exist (Pavlik was killed too young to have children) the nut made a habit of asking every passerby the location of that street. Many pedestrians claimed to have known and tried to remember, but they didn't know the youthful Soviet snitch's fate. Some myths, apparently, do pass.

The bank guard thinks that Russia can never become like California or Germany. "She's too moral to become Hollywood and too *naturally* disorderly to become Berlin." Andrey's views are widely shared. When asked "What is to be done?" the ritual question in Russia, he, like any number of taxi drivers, bus chauffeurs, university guards, and technical staffers, said, "We are not natural democrats. We need a strong master." Putin has lots of male support.

I never heard a Russian *woman* make this argument. Whether believers or not, most of the Russian women with whom I spoke assumed that their intense labor was a traditional duty, seemed not to think in terms of "masters" of any sort. Although I have earlier dismissed the value of public utterance, I will make an exception here for a presentation on Orthodoxy made by a friend, Olga Martinovna, because it bore upon the subject at hand: authority.

As Olga began her lecture for the American students, I remembered that Dimitry Obolensky, a famous historian of Byzantium, described the Orthodox church building as a microcosm, a model of the cosmos, of the spiritual world in which the Orthodox live. In that building, then, said Olga, all stand to worship, sometimes all night, as at Easter, because the body must be kept in proper subjection. Still, this does not necessarily suggest the absolute denigration of the flesh. The food we eat is planted according to the Orthodox calendar. In the making of icons the icon painter supplies the fleshly hand through which God inscribes the linden wood "canvas." Without that fleshly hand, as without the stone ground pigments used in egg tempera, there could be no image. That is, these holy pictures depend upon earthly matter even as they supersede it. The three kisses of greeting, or farewell, the last full on the mouth and representing the Holy Spirit, are meant to heal the mortal flesh. Indeed, the verb "to kiss," *tselovat*, is a calque from *salutare*, to make whole, to make well. For the Orthodox, then, the spirit is close, contiguous, not a separate region of experience, not a threatening authority but a component part of them.

By a fairly obvious association of ideas, I thought of two burn victims with whom I have come into contact here. The first, Monica, is a young American woman in Krasnodar on her own studying Russian. After a number of encounters with plastic surgery, she has again something in the nature of a face, rather like one of those beautiful, distant and stiff masks for the carnival at Venice. Since Monica courses gallantly through life as though on horseback, I guess she has been "kissed." Then there is the man standing in the mud of the East Market, his face melted like uneven lava, blind, silently holding out a hand for alms. There is not the slightest chance that he will ever encounter plastic surgery in Russia, as Russia is now, and yet, a woman carrying a mop and pail in one hand, carefully leading him by the arm with the other, brings him to the market in the early morning and collects him about five p.m. From her look of infinite fondness, I rather think that he, too, has been kissed. This is not, then, your run-of-the-mill sort of problem-solving, but maybe that's what Olga means by "orthodoxy," the authority of the heart.

There is another very present sort of authority in Russia besides the traditions of Orthodoxy and tyranny, "he gave more" and "a strong master." This authority is expressed in the traditional, by no means solely academic, veneration of the classical Russian writers. Reverence for Russia's golden age is national, not merely intellectual The slim counter woman who usually fried my lunch eggs at "Under the Linden Trees" was easily able to cap any Pushkin quote of mine.

Let me give a more thorough example. It happened that our group was scheduled for a weekend visit to Taman, a famous site from Lermontov's novel, *A Hero of Our Time*. The limestone hut where the writer once stayed in the 1830s, depicted in the work as a den of "innocent smugglers" who are dispersed by the autistic machinations of the "hero," Pechorin, does not seem that different from most of Taman's present-day houses. A separate, much larger museum building contains portraits, Lermontov's own landscape paintings, manuscripts and testimonials to the man's genius, not unlike the contents of the museum-homes at Tolstoy's and Turgenev's estates. Our guide related, and I translated, the short life and early death in a duel of this second, after Pushkin, of Russia's poets. The life included a dream that Lermontov is said to have had of his Scottish ancestor, Learmont, and the assertion that a sketch made by Lermontov of his dream ancestor turned out to be a very close likeness of the portrait of that ancestor still preserved in a Scottish castle.

I am struck by the essentially religious piety with which this, and the rest of the life, was narrated. This was hagiography, not literary scholarship. As the Orthodox among the Russians venerate icons, so, also, the great literary figures are revered. In spite of much hard evidence to the contrary, our local guide encouraged us to see Lermontov as a fallen angel, his own "Demon" perhaps, murdered in a duel, like Pushkin, by the forces of black reaction. A simplistic approach, but this adoration of a *literary* figure - almost any literary figure - sets Russian readers apart from American ones. I remember a Leningrad librarian in 1961 who showed me, as a great favor, the poet Esenin's death mask, which she kept in her desk. It is hard to imagine a book like the recent American one exposing F. Scott Fitzgerald as an importunate drunk being written in Russia.

There are, I believe, various reasons for this. Both church and state have, traditionally, censored Russian publication. Only *belles lettres* were somewhat free because they are difficult to censor, based as they often are on suggestion and nuance, what the intelligentsia came to describe as Aesopian language. There is, I have come to see, another basis for the universal admiration of writers such as Pushkin and Lermontov, Turgenev, Dostoevsky, and Tolstoy. Though not one of them was, strictly orthodox, not even Dostoevsky, the central value in their works is just my Natasha's belief that he who gives more loves more. If one reviews the protagonists of their primary works: Onegin, Pechorin, Bazarov, Raskolnikov or Prince Andrey, it becomes apparent that all suffer from a "Western" willfulness, a desire for self-aggrandizement, which is their fatal flaw. In these same works, it is the female protagonists, like Tolstoy's Natasha Rostov, who embody Russian acceptance and forgiveness. That is, Russia's most honored writers celebrate the seemingly hopeless instinct to meet self-willed authority with forgiveness and love. A poem of Lermontov's expresses the attitude of all these artists.

Motherland

I love my Motherland, but with a queer, rogue ardor;

crass common sense must quail before this love.

For neither glory, bought with slaughter,

nor full assurance of proud belief,

nor the dark past's sacred, inviolable tradition

can rouse in me joyous, groundless conviction.

Still I must love – feeling, not knowing why –

Her brooding steppes' cold, silent desolation,

her swaying forest's boundless susurration,

her rivers' springtime floods, like newborn seas.

A back road route I gladly gallop in a cart,

erect, with patient glance enduring night's long dark

to meet, just when I ache for rest, on some chance edge

the trembling lights of her sad villages.

I love the smoke of reaped, burned fallow,

a trader's sparse camp in the gorse

and on a yellow, hilly meadow,

a shining stand of girlish birch.

With joy to many all unknown,

I sight a barn filled full 'fore frost,

a hut capped by a low straw dome

- its windows framed with axe-carved spruce -

and, holidays, 'spite frost's white bite,

I'll hear and watch 'til black midnight

dancing, shrill whistles, shouts and stamps

of garrulous, drunken peasant-tramps.

(My translation.)

This visit to Taman also gave me the opportunity to test Andrey the bank guard's belief that "real" Russian women are to be found only in a Cossack village. I was not eager for this test. A wrought iron balcony fronted my room in the motel. It was, just then, wreathed in autumn-yellow grape leaves and amber clusters of the fruit. It overlooked the wide, gray-sand Black Sea strand, with the reddish cliffs of the Crimea in the distance. Again, I thought, how did I ever make it this far from Wisconsin? It was hard to leave this lovely landscape to attend a mock wedding performance arranged for us by the local Cossack cultural center.

As *starosta*, "elder," it was my place to accept the wide round loaf sprinkled with salt, the traditional welcoming gift, and to return, more or less wittily - the many toasts at the banquet that followed the performance. The "wedding" went off well, match-maker, dowry-haggling parents and all, and was nicely accompanied by the silvery, keening, utterly true voices of a costumed, mixed choir. The singers looked sixty, particularly the worn-faced women, but were really the fifty-year-olds that they took me, at sixty-three, to be. There was something a bit too honey-dovey about the bride and groom, but that music, those sea-deep droning basses, the arabesques of the women's voices above, simply erased their sentimental image. Then came the feast.

Dinner included gray-black, pearly caviar balanced by a butter rosebud on fine, white bread, borscht, breaded veal, stuffed cabbage, six kinds of honeyed Cossack pastries and endless pitchers of the local wine made of those same amber grapes which framed my balcony's view. Polkas, schottisches and, to me, nameless dances helped to oxidize the flow of wine followed by cool, perfectly round and sweet watermelons. The banquet went on for at least three hours, punctuated by the performances of Cossack dancers squatting and kicking and a traditional Cossack accordionist-clown. Our costumed hosts cheered us on our way, as we piled into the bus for the ride home, laden with gifts of more basketball-sized watermelons and wine. We slept away the three hours back to Krasnodar. Perhaps the bank guard Andrey was thinking of those fine voices, the passionate enjoyment of life expressed in that feast and those dances, when he praised the village women. Certainly our pleasure was largely the gift of their work and charm. Taman left a fine *village* flavor in the mouth.

The aftermath of the feast may have something to add to our picture of Russian authority, too. It was a blow to be dropped in the mud of my boulevard turn-around. An autumn drizzle added to the shock of waking up. As the underpasses have been collapsed for the last five years, one had simply to outrun the constant stream of traffic. Breathing, too, was difficult, as Russian vehicles are all quite innocent of anti-pollution devices, and burn a very low-octane fuel. Still, carrying my now-slippery watermelon, I dashed through the interval separating a bus and an electric tram, made it to my side of the river running with four inches of the watery mud that is a major thoroughfare. I was still buoyed by the Cossack accordion tunes from the dance. However, once I hobbled a dozen steps on my side of the boulevard, favoring a hammer toe which took a beating at the mock-wedding, I heard "Stop, comrade!" The Soviet term, no longer used except by the police, immediately dimmed my remembered pleasure. Something, probably the dregs of the wine, elicited:

"I'm no comrade of yours." I was being accosted by three "special" police in gray uniforms. They were supposed to keep order and reduce the number of muggings in Krasnodar. The regular militiamen, in blue uniforms, direct traffic.

"Papers!"

"I don't carry my passport. One might too easily be mugged for it." This was true, but no compliment to the "specials."

"Come with us!" They escorted me, at a taxi-dodging canter, back across the muddy stream, the insane traffic circle that I had just put behind me, to a covered bus stop. Here their officer presided over a dozen more gray figures.

"Wallet! Briefcase!" He left me my watermelon. Then, he extracted dollars and rubles from the wallet and a hunting knife that was my picnic flatware from the briefcase.

"You are staggering, have alcohol on your breath, lack papers, and are carrying an illegal weapon." His phrase was "cold steel." "Either I keep the money and the knife, or we take you to the sobering-up station." My knife and my credit card were passing from hand to hand among the troops. I think it was mainly the knife, a present from an old friend, that did it. I've always been rather meek with governmental authority, especially police.

"No! I am an American teacher at the university. Give me your badge number, and then we'll both go to the police station. I look forward to explaining to your superior."

"We don't have badge numbers. You may go!"

"Not without my knife and money!" Amazingly, the wallet, bills, and briefcase were returned. Certainly my foreign accent helped.

"Now the knife!"

"But it's an illegal weapon!" Then, more quietly, "Will you sell it?"

"No."

The knife was produced, and I slopped back off through the mud and mad machines of the traffic circle for the third time. One of the gray men even caught up with me to return the forgotten credit card. On my side of the circle again, I resisted the instinct to dribble the watermelon, followed the broken sidewalks to the kiosk behind my apartment-block, bought cigarettes, and complained of my adventure to the young woman on duty. She laughed.

"Those gray cretins! They're up at the circle every Sunday night. They wait for drunks outside the disco, then extort bribes to let them go. They don't touch real alcoholics. Genuine rummies never have any money." Then, the usual, damned *understanding*. "Of course, those specials haven't been paid for months either. They have to do *something*!"

In my kitchen, I set the round watermelon in a cockroach-free corner and thought that those police were rather like Catherine's eighteenth-century Dnieper pirate-Cossacks. Where would Putin find land to commandeer for them? Could they learn to raise watermelons? Finally, "Just like a Russian woman to understand, to make excuses for, to *forgive* those fascist cretins."

My colonel's widow, Irina, the bank guard, Olga and Russian literature itself ought to have been enough to teach me that the essence of this authoritarian society lay, oddly enough, not in self-assertion but in loving forgiveness. I had found the alternative to middle-class order and success that I was seeking when I first came to this country, thirty-six years before, and that alternative was not Marxist but rather, traditionally at least, Orthodox. Being a slow learner, it took my best Russian friend, Tatyana Alexandrovna, to drive the lesson finally, painfully home.

My brightest memory of Tatyana is of a sunny Sunday in a park. I was with Tanya, her sister Nadya, and Nadya's son Anton. It was late on an October afternoon. There was a Ferris wheel, a shooting gallery, a kiosk-restaurant, and a raised dance platform on this overgrown, weedy island in the Kuban river that was once a nobleman's estate.

A Cossack choir in full regalia, cartridge pouches, and all, stood fifty yards from the circular dance pavilion and competed with the bad old rock of a pickup band and its booming, scratchy PA system. The splintered dance floor was so crowded that the dancers could only move up and down, like pistons. Further along the esplanade, on a wide place in the macadam walkway, a group of older dancers, my age, were doing a slow foxtrot to someone's portable tape player. In cheap, fake Panama hats and Soviet style wide-legged trousers a number of suited old men with WWII insignia, military medals in worn, washed-out gray lapels, fox-trotted. Their partners, in worn, broken high heels or even *tapochki*, carpet slippers, their stainless steel teeth sparkling, were enjoying themselves. These older men *and* women tended to be overweight, the women's hair was badly but not recently dyed with henna. Still, they were capable of a stylish twirl on a swollen ankle in a gray, washed out sock. Though Tanya had little patience with their indiscipline, the overweight is not so much the result of gluttony as of a diet of bread and lard or sour cream: both cheap and available. I felt that these were *my* people, ready , thirsty for enjoyment after a tough week. Whether or not they could survive on their laughable pensions, they were stern in the pursuit of joy.

Tanya, a martinet most times, marshaled us for a walk to this park as if she were Patton commanding tanks. I joined forces with her family and muttered, but obeyed. I found, though, that I did have some conscience left, grinned at Tanya, admitted that I'd sit forever over her borscht, but I needed a shove. Out in the tiny hall of her shared apartment, shoes now replacing the "tapochki" (as none are large enough for me, I was allowed to go stocking footed in the house), we were marched toward the park. Another Tanya, Anton's svelte sister, had had a quiet quarrel with her mother Nadya, and now slipped off to meet "those boys," who gave both Nadya and Tanya the shivers.

On the way to the park, Tanya bought beer, Turkish *Efes*, a luxury, for nephew Anton, herself, and me. She had the Russian fear that her guests would perish unless continually supplied with edibles and drinkables. Nadia stuck to Polish 7-Up. We settled on an old oak and cast-iron bench, drank, and Anton smoked a much-frowned-upon cigarette which, nevertheless, Tanya cadged from me for him. I smoked, too, Polish Marlboros. (Everything seemed to be imported but the aforementioned bread and lard.) We, somehow, began a discussion of Nabokov's *Pnin*, a propos, I guess, of my observation of the new, to me, interest in emigration among Russians. Then, we were occupied with Nabokov's translation theories and Pushkin, especially the latter's *The Captain's Daughter* as a late satire on his own *Eugene Onegin*. We debated whether Eugene was a cad or not. We came, finally, to the sources of imagination, what Pushkin called the gift of seeing through your subject's eyes. We might say "wearing his moccasins." As usual, it was an all-night Russian conversation in the afternoon. Nadya, generally the quiet sister, who had been abandoned by her husband, and who still desperately loved the jerk, (her "beautiful," used for both sexes here, gone Georgian) entered strongly on the side of my assertion that jerkdom is to be defined as *using* others. The next minute she defended Onegin for his "beauty." Was there no end to this feminine inconsequence, this borrowing of illicit cigarettes for Anton, this spoiling of men? I absolutely understand why a number of my former students have married Russian women. Who *wouldn't* like to be treated like a pasha?

Mosquitoes finally drove us from our seminar-bench. There was a copse of ebony and silver birches, not native here, brought by settlers from the north and the essence of slim, maidenly beauty, as they are at home in the north. Anton found a bush. No one knowing Russia would go near a public toilet, and there wasn't a trace of American embarrassment. Yesterday a friend of both sisters, a teacher of French, simply couldn't understand why anyone cared with whom Clinton made love. *Right on!*, but hardly U.S. usage, no more so than Anton's cavalier use of a bush.

We took a relaxed sunset stroll all the way around the sizeable birch grove, then back along the shore of the Kuban River. The evening fishermen were placing their setlines for catfish while belated swimmers thrashed ashore. For us it was time to prepare Monday classes, and we went our separate ways. I foolishly attempted to thank Tatyana for the lovely afternoon, but she, American in her unwillingness to accept a compliment, simply ordered me to be early at the department, *kafedra*, tomorrow.

The next Saturday, Anton and I ran into the local "Nazi" leader at the weekly outdoor book sale. The sale was located at the far side of an unkempt, richly autumnal park at the farthest end of the streetcar line. This hardly mattered. Sometimes, I think that I would cross the Gobi desert for a book sale in China, though I'm utterly innocent of Chinese. Sunk in the contemplation of Platonov, Brodsky, even that fine old, Russian, Conan

Doyle, I missed the political highlight of the day. After a sudden rain drove us back to the tram early, Anton entertained me with a description of the appearance of the chief local Nazi, in fatigues, beret, and swastikas, at the book market. Living between old pages, I completely missed this. Bemused police walked this local *Führer* out of the park to avoid attack by book lovers, saying, "We must have missed this one during the war." Whatever his own racial views, Anton feared the mindless, cold passion of these *Russian* Nazis, especially because his sister, young Tatyana, had been known to hang out at the soccer stadium with other swingers, and that was also where the local Nazis met. It was these skinheads' loudly expressed desire to kill everyone, Jews first, that is not of pure Russian blood.

Back at Tatyana's apartment, Nadya took up the racism: "Pure? After two thousand years of drunken promiscuity and invasions from east and west? Pure?"

She looked a bit like a nun, this lonely abandoned mom, though she bloomed on weekends away from her wash pail job. (The brick works that she managed was closed.) She had spunk and could match Tatyana's sharp tongue when provoked. Having visited her former husband's family, she loved Georgia, the many-voiced men's singing, and the snowy mountains. This attraction, Nadya and I shared.

Tatyana said that Nadya's rat-husband left not because he was a Georgian, "Georgians take care of their families," but because he was half-Ukrainian, a mongrel. I: "That's racism!" Tatyana: "It's true, though racist." Still, the next week, having met him there on Stavropol Street, sick and sad at the death of his mother, she forgave him his treatment of Nadya and lent him some money. Russian women!

Though I had my own atrociously spacious three rooms, Tatyana's communal parlor and half-kitchen were practically my second home. As she could not afford to buy her apartment when Russians were, after socialism, given this opportunity, she slept in her parlor and shared the kitchen, bath, and hall with an older man who lived in a bedroom that also served as *his* parlor. Tatyana alone paid for the steel door that is now, since socialism, a feature of all but the poorest apartments. Oleg, her apartment-mate, claimed he couldn't help pay. Tatyana took it out of Oleg in the small change of plumbing or electrical repairs, at which he was, not very skilled. Now a single woman of thirty-seven, a fine, inventive language teacher, an utter giver I thought her then and think her still. She made a habit of teaching the weakest of our students and tutored my own Sarah and David when they were eleven and nine. Betraying no knowledge of English, of which she had, indeed, a solid, active grasp, she taught my kids the cruel complexities of Russian verbs of motion with rubber balls and thrown playing cards, *infected* them with the desire to speak to her, to please her. She became for them, I suspect, Russia itself: giving, never still, gay in a dark and sparkling way, like some ambers, with unlimited vitality. In the absence of decent texts, Tatyana wrote her own. She kept a day ahead of her classes who became, in their turn, dedicated scholars of Russian. She seemed unaffected by squalid surroundings. She professed no formal faith. I think that she was, in a very Orthodox way, dependent upon adversity, lost without its challenge, its opportunity to give more.

In 1991, when I first worked at Kuban State University, the Soviet Union was collapsing after the kidnapping of Gorbachev and the Army's refusal to fire on Yeltsin's "White House." During that chaotic time, Tatyana lost her position as head teacher for our American group. Now, seven years later, the old chair had died, and Tatyana was head teacher for us again. She was, however, looked down upon for losing the university money by helping Michael, the previous year's director of the American group, to arrange the annual tour of Moscow and St. Petersburg through a private firm rather than through the university. Nevertheless, though she could no longer act as official assistant, Tatyana fed me, initiated me into university politics, and became, in a way, my sister. *Her* sister, nephew, Anton, and niece, Tatyana, formed a family group into which I was cordially accepted. This meant, as always in Russia, a great danger of overeating. I did not come to Tatyana's parlor with *empty hands*, as the Russians say, but, of course, my wine and flowers, beef and bread, in no way paid for friendship. It was a rare week on Stavropol Street, when I didn't inhale my evening borscht and kasha more often at Tatyana's table than at my own.

The portions of university politics that accompanied the dinners were less palatable. Tatyana's *kafedra*, now chaired by Luisa, an *Amerikanist*, had the new title of "Center for American Studies," and Luisa had pretensions to a budget separate from that of the university. The Rector did not and could not agree. He was, at this time, in a position to pay, at most, sixty percent, one hundred dollars, of the official average monthly salary. Luisa, who had the patronage of my American sponsors, expected him to pay higher salaries to the teachers of her Center. This led to bad feeling in the other *kafedras.*

A further and, ultimately disastrous wrinkle was Ira, executive head of the office for foreign students, who saw herself as defender of university interests. Ira was in charge of a budget for ballet performances, jazz concerts and dinners to entertain foreign students. She did her best to force me to pay for such things out of a fund I brought along for student educational extras. Ira was further responsible to book individual and return travel for my American group, arrange for the renewal of visas, and see to medical treatment for injured or ailing foreign students. As she was often absent from her office, arranged for visas late or not at all until pushed, and attacked the students' Russian hosts when *they* did not assume *her* medical responsibilities, I found myself all too frequently in the position of doing her work or making fruitless attempts to find her when some health or travel crisis developed.

The difficulties suggested above were all, more or less, bearable. Unfortunately, Ira was also the person through whom I felt forced to arrange my group's two-week tour of Moscow and St. Petersburg, a major aspect of our Russian program. As Ira attempted to have Tatyana fired for assisting the previous American director in this matter, I found myself at Ira's mercy in the organization of the tour. She tended to think in terms of visits to the zoo, jazz concerts, and inspections of television stations. I promoted high culture: museums and historical monuments. We also disagreed about allowable expenses, Ira at one time arriving at a figure for the tour that was double my whole semester budget. Although I met with her three times a week for eight weeks about tour arrangements, and she dealt, she said, with two different private travel companies, important negative changes in plan were still occurring on the eve of our departure for Moscow. Suddenly we were moved to a hotel far from central Moscow, for instance, and at several points meals for the group were not supplied.

A quiet, intelligent university associate of Ira's who followed the vicissitudes of my business with her from some distance, surprised me one day by calling Ira a "furious bitch." He said that Ira was of the sort noted in Gogol's "Overcoat" who "kick only those who can't bite." Americans she slobbered over, and used, if possible. Russians she kicked around, if they were essentially defenseless. She worked both lazily and inefficiently.

There is, finally, a reason for this unpleasant explanation. When, after seemingly endless delay, we actually reached Moscow on our tour, neither Ira nor the official guide could find our distant hotel. Tatyana, who came prepared with a city map, found it. At the hotel, dinner was less than insufficient, a waiter attempted to blackmail us when we requested extra bread, and the time wasted finding the hotel made the city orientation tour so short as to be useless. Ira, whose duty it was to defend our interests, did nothing at all. I threw a tantrum, my third or fourth over the years in Russia. Food got somewhat more abundant and at no extra cost. The city tour was lengthened. Ira was jogged sufficiently to begin to keep track of the students when they got on and off of the bus. Still, as you will see, this is not a tale of my wisdom or mastery, but of loss.

The next day, a lovely, snowy, Zhivago sort of day, Ira and I met her "friend," a scalper or "wolf," to bargain for tickets to the Bolshoi Ballet. "Wolves" buy up these tickets, still government subsidized, and resell them at something like New York prices, to tourists. We bought thirteen tickets. From the wolf's bad chart of the seating in the Bolshoi Theater, it was impossible to check locations. The Bolshoi Theater itself had "lost" its seating chart. In the midst of these festivities, police with a camcorder approached. Ira, who had just gotten tickets for herself and her son, at considerably lower prices, and I were allowed to depart with our tickets. Conversations with other scalpers led me to believe that the police simply skimmed off fifty percent of our wolf's profit.

At this point, Ira, who arrived late for our date with the scalper, offered to distribute the ballet tickets to the students, as they arrived that evening at the Bolshoi Theater. At this time, the students were all over downtown Moscow exploring on their own so her idea seemed reasonable. I found myself seeing eight very nicely dressed young ladies off to their first Russian ballet from our distant hotel. I had also the distinct disappointment of meeting them when they returned, some in tears, some furious, an hour and a half later. Ira had not met them with the tickets. I became angry for real.

When Ira and her son returned from the ballet, she said that the students had not arrived in time. The students said that they arrived ten minutes before the curtain was to go up. Now, the Bolshoi Theater has always been strict about such matters, but my reading of the situation, based, of course, on my history with Ira, was that she abandoned the students to be sure of a place for herself and her son. A genuine teacher, as Tatyana and her colleague Irina Viktorovna agreed, would have risked missing the ballet on the off chance, quite likely, really, of talking, or bribing, the students into the Bolshoi at the last second. Enraged, I decided to send the useless Ira back to Krasnodar.

Now, the long-delayed point of the story. Tatyana, who suffered Ira's tyranny for years, almost lost her teaching position because of Ira's complaints, and kept me current on the monster's more immediate crimes, now violently attacked *me* for my decision. "Ira, as a mother, cannot afford to lose her position! It is your religious duty to forgive her!"

I buckled. I agreed to allow Ira to finish the tour. Still, I promised to do my best to have her replaced so that next year's director wouldn't have the daily frustration of dealing with her. Ira, in her turn, threatened to inform the Rector that I was a senile drunk. Tatyana, ultimately, told me that I was insane, "spiritually ill," as the psyche and the soul are one to Russians and exiled me from her presence and parlor.

Tatyana, from her perspective, was absolutely right. Though no regular communicant, she is essentially Orthodox, a Christian, as I am not, as Protestants and Catholics generally are not. For the Orthodox, and how often I have experienced this, giving and forgiveness as a kind of giving is the one absolutely necessary virtue. Without suffering and the forgiveness that suffering occasions, Orthodox life would be meaningless. All other views, when examined closely, are, for the Orthodox, "spiritual madness."

I never ate another bowl of Tatyana's borscht and never saw her sister Nadya again. I was, thank goodness, kept somewhat in touch by nephew Anton, a self-confessed Nietzschean, but remained utterly cast off by Tatyana, my Russian "sister." Ira was said to have lost her position. Tatyana is said to have quit hers.

It is, no doubt, an honor for a "German," a *nemets,* to be judged by Orthodox standards. I'd rather eat Tatyana's borscht.

For the last month before returning to the States to consider the "spiritual madness" of which Tatyana accused me, I met my student wards every morning at nine and spent the days attempting to arrange the exit visas for which Ira had forgotten to apply. I visited classes, intervened with students and teachers when some academic "injustice," usually a grade, loomed. Still, the first two hours of every morning, I spent walking through, across, and around the grove of silver-gray birches in Tatyana's Sunday park. Perhaps I came to some conclusions and reached *understanding,* if that is possible, while still walking *mother raw earth,* the original Russian godhead.

December eleventh was my last Krasnodar day. To come to those wise, pliant birches to which Tatyana introduced me, I paced, in early light, a bridge across an arm of the Kuban River, watched fisherman-pensioners pull up their mostly fishless nets, nodded to gray-headed joggers and patted, gingerly, a few of the hundreds of homeless dogs that infest Krasnodar like the drunks. Then I passed the fading, flaking Ferris wheel, Dodg'em cars, shooting gallery, and children's train of the now largely derelict amusement park. Such joys, which implied a concern for children, for the future, had always been a prominent feature of the murderous Soviet state, witness Dzerzhinsky's concern for orphans. In its decay, the park seemed particularly pathetic. I walked southeast along the central boulevard of the park between bent and tipped benches and little-used waste receptacles in the form of classical columns. In this way I arrived at the birches.

I thought much about Tatyana, who had sometimes curled up like a kitten with her sister Nadya on the parlor couch, while nephew Anton and I chewed doggedly at our endless discussion of altruism in Dostoevsky, or Anton unloaded yet another barely decent, fairly scabrous anecdote. I heard, those December mornings, mental echoes of it.

All these sensory memories brought back earlier idle thoughts of resettling here in Krasnodar, finding work at the university, finishing out my time in Russia. However, my "spiritual madness," the attempt *to change a hurtful reality at another mortal's expense*, that is, my decision to fire Ira, mother or not, had quashed that ill-founded plan. I am no Russian. I am not Orthodox. I cannot always leave justice, that proud word, to God, though I know that I, too, am unjust.

I remembered, also, a demonstration in St. Petersburg on the anniversary of the October Revolution, this very year of 1997. There were three thousand ill-dressed workers, and the procession was led by two men holding up a large picture of Lenin and an older woman played the International on a wheezy accordion. Crude, cruel placards blamed "the Zionists, the Jews" for capitalism's present rough grip on Russia, which feels very much like brigandage and theft. I spoke then with a Jewish couple in the crowd of spectators. Their small daughter listened, as they debated flight to Finland, which is close, but where they knew no one, and Poland, where they had friends, but which was relatively far to go. This flight was to occur, if and when the now "fascist" Communist party, just then passing us with its placards, should indeed gain serious political power. These well-spoken intellectuals told me that the present demonstration, near the Alexander I column on Palace Square, was more about unpaid wages than politics. Nevertheless, it was exactly the Jews, my present co-conversationalists, who were again being blamed for Russia's immemorial ills. I thought of this under the birches, too, probably because it seemed an injustice which Orthodoxy allowed for far too long.

Since my return from Krasnodar, I have read Fedotov's *The Russian Religious Mind* and accepted his view of the ancient and widespread nature in Russia, of *kenotic* Christianity, the acceptance of suffering as an imitation of Christ, along with an innocent ignorance of any other religious possibility. The self-sacrificing generosity, which I have for forty-five years enjoyed in this country, may be grounded on this *kenosis*. Its strict teachings state that suffering replaces justice and is to be accepted as grace, and that those who seek justice too energetically are spiritually mad, are usurping divine authority.

When I sought to fire Ira, I was drawing upon a literary, but hardly Christian, source. I saw Ira, a quintessential "New Russian," as the soul sister of that insufferable Natasha who irresistibly drives Nina, Masha, and Olga from their home in Chekhov's *Three Sisters*. Russian audiences have always wept at the conclusion of that play, as they wept at the end of *The Cherry Orchard*, even in Soviet times, even when those displaced were the class enemy; but for me, as for Chekhov, weeping is not enough, I cannot turn the other cheek: I am not a Russian. All this I thought among the silver birches of Tatyana's island-park.

Still, it was there, that last cold December morning, that I saw one of the joggers clutching, embracing, like a *leshy*, a forest demon, the snow-white, silver-shining trunk of a birch, and staring at the ruin of the amusement park. He looked right through me. He had all Russia's long-suffering to support him. He was stronger than I.

WORKS CITED

Camus, Albert *Tagebücher 1935-1951* 1982

Chatwin, Bruce *The Song Lines* 1986

Djilas, Milovan *The New* Class 1982

Fedotov, George P. *The Russian Religious Mind* 1975

Gogol, Nikolai *The Overcoat* 1842

Gogol, Nikolai *Nevsky Prospekt* 2008

Kuraev, Mixail *Night Patrol and Other Stories* 1994

Le Carré, John *The Russia House* 1989

Le Guin, Ursula, *Dancing at the Edge of the World* 1989

Lermontov, Mixail *A Hero of Our Time*

Lermontov, Mixail *Stichovoreniya* 1940

Opolovnikov, A.V. *Kizhi* 1970

Pasternak, Boris *Dr. Zhivago* 1957

Pushkin, A. S. *Sobraniye Sochinyenyi* 1967

Richards, Susan *Epics of Everyday Life* 1992

Rilke, Rainer Maria *Die Weise von Liebe und Tod des Cornets Christopher Rilke* 1906

Sinyavsky, Andrei *A Voice from the Chorus* 1973

Smiley, Jane *MOO* 1995

West, Rebecca *Black Lamb and Grey Falcon. A Journey...* 1941

CPSIA information can be obtained at www.ICGtesting.com
Printed in the USA
LVOW12s0904261113

362782LV00003B/260/P